Y0-BPT-342

WITHDRAWN

EX LIBRIS

SOUTH ORANGE
PUBLIC LIBRARY

ALEXANDER DUBČEK

ALEXANDER DUBČEK

Ina Navazelskis

CHELSEA HOUSE PUBLISHERS
NEW YORK
PHILADELPHIA

Chelsea House Publishers
EDITOR-IN-CHIEF: Remmel Nunn
MANAGING EDITOR: Karyn Gullen Browne
COPY CHIEF: Juliann Barbato
PICTURE EDITOR: Adrian G. Allen
ART DIRECTOR: Maria Epes
DEPUTY COPY CHIEF: Mark Rifkin
ASSISTANT ART DIRECTOR: Loraine Machlin
MANUFACTURING MANAGER: Gerald Levine
SYSTEMS MANAGER: Rachel Vigier
PRODUCTION MANAGER: Joseph Romano
PRODUCTION COORDINATOR: Marie Claire Cebrián

World Leaders—Past & Present
SENIOR EDITOR: John W. Selfridge

Staff for ALEXANDER DUBČEK
COPY EDITOR: Philip Koslow
PICTURE RESEARCHER: Andrea Reithmayr
DESIGNER: David Murray
COVER ILLUSTRATION: Eileen McKeating

Copyright © 1990 by Chelsea House Publishers, a division of
Main Line Book Co. All rights reserved. Printed and bound in
the United States of America.

First Printing

1 3 5 7 9 8 6 4 2

Library of Congress Cataloging-in-Publication Data

Navazelskis, Ina L.
  Alexander Dubček/by Ina Navazelskis.
  p.   cm.—(World leaders past & present)
  Includes bibliographical references.
  Summary: Follows the life of the Czechoslovakian leader.
  ISBN 1-55546-831-4
        0-7910-0674-3 (pbk.)
  1. Dubček, Alexander, 1921–   —Juvenile literature.
2. Statesmen—Czechoslovakia—Biography—Juvenile literature.
[1. Dubček, Alexander, 1921–   . 2. Statesmen.] I. Title. II. Series.
DB2221. D83N38   1990
943.704′092—dc20   90–1758
[B]   CIP
[92]   AC

Contents

WORLD LEADERS PAST & PRESENT

John Adams
John Quincy Adams
Konrad Adenauer
Alexander the Great
Salvador Allende
Marc Antony
Corazon Aquino
Yasir Arafat
King Arthur
Hafez al-Assad
Kemal Atatürk
Attila
Clement Attlee
Augustus Caesar
Menachem Begin
David Ben-Gurion
Otto von Bismarck
Léon Blum
Simon Bolívar
Cesare Borgia
Willy Brandt
Leonid Brezhnev
Julius Caesar
John Calvin
Jimmy Carter
Fidel Castro
Catherine the Great
Charlemagne
Chiang Kai-Shek
Winston Churchill
Georges Clemenceau
Cleopatra
Constantine the Great
Hernán Cortés
Oliver Cromwell
Georges-Jacques
    Danton
Jefferson Davis
Moshe Dayan
Charles de Gaulle
Eamon De Valera
Eugene Debs
Deng Xiaoping
Benjamin Disraeli
Alexander Dubček
François & Jean-Claude
    Duvalier
Dwight Eisenhower
Eleanor of Aquitaine
Elizabeth I
Faisal
Ferdinand & Isabella
Francisco Franco
Benjamin Franklin

Frederick the Great
Indira Gandhi
Mohandas Gandhi
Giuseppe Garibaldi
Amin & Bashir Gemayel
Genghis Khan
William Gladstone
Mikhail Gorbachev
Ulysses S. Grant
Ernesto "Che" Guevara
Tenzin Gyatso
Alexander Hamilton
Dag Hammarskjöld
Henry VIII
Henry of Navarre
Paul von Hindenburg
Hirohito
Adolf Hitler
Ho Chi Minh
King Hussein
Ivan the Terrible
Andrew Jackson
James I
Wojciech Jaruzelski
Thomas Jefferson
Joan of Arc
Pope John XXIII
Pope John Paul II
Lyndon Johnson
Benito Juárez
John Kennedy
Robert Kennedy
Jomo Kenyatta
Ayatollah Khomeini
Nikita Khrushchev
Kim Il Sung
Martin Luther King, Jr.
Henry Kissinger
Kublai Khan
Lafayette
Robert E. Lee
Vladimir Lenin
Abraham Lincoln
David Lloyd George
Louis XIV
Martin Luther
Judas Maccabeus
James Madison
Nelson & Winnie
    Mandela
Mao Zedong
Ferdinand Marcos
George Marshall

Mary, Queen of Scots
Tomáš Masaryk
Golda Meir
Klemens von Metternich
James Monroe
Hosni Mubarak
Robert Mugabe
Benito Mussolini
Napoléon Bonaparte
Gamal Abdel Nasser
Jawaharlal Nehru
Nero
Nicholas II
Richard Nixon
Kwame Nkrumah
Daniel Ortega
Mohammed Reza Pahlavi
Thomas Paine
Charles Stewart
    Parnell
Pericles
Juan Perón
Peter the Great
Pol Pot
Muammar el-Qaddafi
Ronald Reagan
Cardinal Richelieu
Maximilien Robespierre
Eleanor Roosevelt
Franklin Roosevelt
Theodore Roosevelt
Anwar Sadat
Haile Selassie
Prince Sihanouk
Jan Smuts
Joseph Stalin
Sukarno
Sun Yat-sen
Tamerlane
Mother Teresa
Margaret Thatcher
Josip Broz Tito
Toussaint L'Ouverture
Leon Trotsky
Pierre Trudeau
Harry Truman
Queen Victoria
Lech Walesa
George Washington
Chaim Weizmann
Woodrow Wilson
Xerxes
Emiliano Zapata
Zhou Enlai

CHELSEA HOUSE PUBLISHERS

ON LEADERSHIP

Arthur M. Schlesinger, jr.

LEADERSHIP, it may be said, is really what makes the world go round. Love no doubt smooths the passage; but love is a private transaction between consenting adults. Leadership is a public transaction with history. The idea of leadership affirms the capacity of individuals to move, inspire, and mobilize masses of people so that they act together in pursuit of an end. Sometimes leadership serves good purposes, sometimes bad; but whether the end is benign or evil, great leaders are those men and women who leave their personal stamp on history.

Now, the very concept of leadership implies the proposition that individuals can make a difference. This proposition has never been universally accepted. From classical times to the present day, eminent thinkers have regarded individuals as no more than the agents and pawns of larger forces, whether the gods and goddesses of the ancient world or, in the modern era, race, class, nation, the dialectic, the will of the people, the spirit of the times, history itself. Against such forces, the individual dwindles into insignificance.

So contends the thesis of historical determinism. Tolstoy's great novel *War and Peace* offers a famous statement of the case. Why, Tolstoy asked, did millions of men in the Napoleonic Wars, denying their human feelings and their common sense, move back and forth across Europe slaughtering their fellows? "The war," Tolstoy answered, "was bound to happen simply because it was bound to happen." All prior history predetermined it. As for leaders, they, Tolstoy said, "are but the labels that serve to give a name to an end and, like labels, they have the least possible connection with the event." The greater the leader, "the more conspicuous the inevitability and the predestination of every act he commits." The leader, said Tolstoy, is "the slave of history."

Determinism takes many forms. Marxism is the determinism of class. Nazism the determinism of race. But the idea of men and women as the slaves of history runs athwart the deepest human instincts. Rigid determinism abolishes the idea of human freedom—

the assumption of free choice that underlies every move we make, every word we speak, every thought we think. It abolishes the idea of human responsibility, since it is manifestly unfair to reward or punish people for actions that are by definition beyond their control. No one can live consistently by any deterministic creed. The Marxist states prove this themselves by their extreme susceptibility to the cult of leadership.

More than that, history refutes the idea that individuals make no difference. In December 1931 a British politician crossing Park Avenue in New York City between 76th and 77th Streets around 10:30 P.M. looked in the wrong direction and was knocked down by an automobile—a moment, he later recalled, of a man aghast, a world aglare: "I do not understand why I was not broken like an eggshell or squashed like a gooseberry." Fourteen months later an American politician, sitting in an open car in Miami, Florida, was fired on by an assassin; the man beside him was hit. Those who believe that individuals make no difference to history might well ponder whether the next two decades would have been the same had Mario Constasino's car killed Winston Churchill in 1931 and Giuseppe Zangara's bullet killed Franklin Roosevelt in 1933. Suppose, in addition, that Adolf Hitler had been killed in the street fighting during the Munich *Putsch* of 1923 and that Lenin had died of typhus during World War I. What would the 20th century be like now?

For better or for worse, individuals do make a difference. "The notion that a people can run itself and its affairs anonymously," wrote the philosopher William James, "is now well known to be the silliest of absurdities. Mankind does nothing save through initiatives on the part of inventors, great or small, and imitation by the rest of us—these are the sole factors in human progress. Individuals of genius show the way, and set the patterns, which common people then adopt and follow."

Leadership, James suggests, means leadership in thought as well as in action. In the long run, leaders in thought may well make the greater difference to the world. But, as Woodrow Wilson once said, "Those only are leaders of men, in the general eye, who lead in action. . . . It is at their hands that new thought gets its trans-lation into the crude language of deeds." Leaders in thought often invent in solitude and obscurity, leaving to later generations the tasks of imitation. Leaders in action—the leaders portrayed in this series—have to be effective in their own time.

And they cannot be effective by themselves. They must act in response to the rhythms of their age. Their genius must be adapted, in a phrase of William James's, "to the receptivities of the moment." Leaders are useless without followers. "There goes the mob," said the French politician hearing a clamor in the streets. "I am their leader. I must follow them." Great leaders turn the inchoate emotions of the mob to purposes of their own. They seize on the opportunities of their time, the hopes, fears, frustrations, crises, potentialities. They succeed when events have prepared the way for them, when the community is awaiting to be aroused, when they can provide the clarifying and organizing ideas. Leadership ignites the circuit between the individual and the mass and thereby alters history.

It may alter history for better or for worse. Leaders have been responsible for the most extravagant follies and most monstrous crimes that have beset suffering humanity. They have also been vital in such gains as humanity has made in individual freedom, religious and racial tolerance, social justice, and respect for human rights.

There is no sure way to tell in advance who is going to lead for good and who for evil. But a glance at the gallery of men and women in *World Leaders—Past and Present* suggests some useful tests.

One test is this: Do leaders lead by force or by persuasion? By command or by consent? Through most of history leadership was exercised by the divine right of authority. The duty of followers was to defer and to obey. "Theirs not to reason why / Theirs but to do and die." On occasion, as with the so-called enlightened despots of the 18th century in Europe, absolutist leadership was animated by humane purposes. More often, absolutism nourished the passion for domination, land, gold, and conquest and resulted in tyranny.

The great revolution of modern times has been the revolution of equality. The idea that all people should be equal in their legal condition has undermined the old structure of authority, hierarchy, and deference. The revolution of equality has had two contrary effects on the nature of leadership. For equality, as Alexis de Tocqueville pointed out in his great study *Democracy in America*, might mean equality in servitude as well as equality in freedom.

"I know of only two methods of establishing equality in the political world," Tocqueville wrote. "Rights must be given to every citizen, or none at all to anyone . . . save one, who is the master of all." There was no middle ground "between the sovereignty of all and the absolute power of one man." In his astonishing prediction of 20th-century totalitarian dictatorship, Tocqueville explained how the revolution of equality could lead to the *"Führerprinzip"* and more terrible absolutism than the world had ever known.

But when rights are given to every citizen and the sovereignty of all is established, the problem of leadership takes a new form, becomes more exacting than ever before. It is easy to issue commands and enforce them by the rope and the stake, the concentration camp and the *gulag.* It is much harder to use argument and achievement to overcome opposition and win consent. The Founding Fathers of the United States understood the difficulty. They believed that history had given them the opportunity to decide, as Alexander Hamilton wrote in the first Federalist Paper, whether men are indeed capable of basing government on "reflection and choice, or whether they are forever destined to depend . . . on accident and force."

Government by reflection and choice called for a new style of leadership and a new quality of followership. It required leaders to be responsive to popular concerns, and it required followers to be active and informed participants in the process. Democracy does not eliminate emotion from politics; sometimes it fosters demagoguery; but it is confident that, as the greatest of democratic leaders put it, you cannot fool all of the people all of the time. It measures leadership by results and retires those who overreach or falter or fail.

It is true that in the long run despots are measured by results too. But they can postpone the day of judgment, sometimes indefinitely, and in the meantime they can do infinite harm. It is also true that democracy is no guarantee of virtue and intelligence in government, for the voice of the people is not necessarily the voice of God. But democracy, by assuring the right of opposition, offers built-in resistance to the evils inherent in absolutism. As the theologian Reinhold Niebuhr summed it up, "Man's capacity for justice makes democracy possible, but man's inclination to injustice makes democracy necessary."

A second test for leadership is the end for which power is sought. When leaders have as their goal the supremacy of a master race or the promotion of totalitarian revolution or the acquisition and exploitation of colonies or the protection of greed and privilege or the preservation of personal power, it is likely that their leadership will do little to advance the cause of humanity. When their goal is the abolition of slavery, the liberation of women, the enlargement of opportunity for the poor and powerless, the extension of equal rights to racial minorities, the defense of the freedoms of expression and opposition, it is likely that their leadership will increase the sum of human liberty and welfare.

Leaders have done great harm to the world. They have also conferred great benefits. You will find both sorts in this series. Even "good" leaders must be regarded with a certain wariness. Leaders are not demigods; they put on their trousers one leg after another just like ordinary mortals. No leader is infallible, and every leader needs to be reminded of this at regular intervals. Irreverence irritates leaders but is their salvation. Unquestioning submission corrupts leaders and demeans followers. Making a cult of a leader is always a mistake. Fortunately hero worship generates its own antidote. "Every hero," said Emerson, "becomes a bore at last."

The signal benefit the great leaders confer is to embolden the rest of us to live according to our own best selves, to be active, insistent, and resolute in affirming our own sense of things. For great leaders attest to the reality of human freedom against the supposed inevitabilities of history. And they attest to the wisdom and power that may lie within the most unlikely of us, which is why Abraham Lincoln remains the supreme example of great leadership. A great leader, said Emerson, exhibits new possibilities to all humanity. "We feed on genius. . . . Great men exist that there may be greater men."

Great leaders, in short, justify themselves by emancipating and empowering their followers. So humanity struggles to master its destiny, remembering with Alexis de Tocqueville: "It is true that around every man a fatal circle is traced beyond which he cannot pass; but within the wide verge of that circle he is powerful and free; as it is with man, so with communities."

1

The Dream

In November 1989, a tall man wearing a gray business suit, his thinning silver hair brushed away from his forehead, stood on a balcony in Prague, Czechoslovakia, smiling down on an enormous crowd that had gathered in the capital city's Wenceslas Square. Just days away from his 68th birthday, Alexander Dubček was a national hero. He gazed over the crowd of 350,000 cheering demonstrators, many of whom chanted "Long Live Dubček!" and carried signs that read Dubček: President! Moving to the edge of the balcony, Dubček threw his arms open wide and symbolically embraced the crowd of demonstrators, and the people roared their approval.

Some 20 years before, as first secretary of the Czechoslovak Communist party, Dubček was the leader of Czechoslovakia. His warm and humble nature had made him the country's most trusted leader in more than 40 years of Communist rule. Now, though he had been absent from public life for more than two decades, Dubček was remembered and still loved by the Czechoslovak people.

In everyone there is some longing for humanity's rightful dignity, for moral integrity, for free expression of being and a sense of transcendence over the world of existence.
—VÁCLAV HAVEL
Czech playwright
and leader of the
democracy movement,
January 1, 1990

The dissident playwright Václav Havel (right) hugs former Czechoslovak president Alexander Dubček on November 24, 1989, following the resignation of the entire Czechoslovak government. Popular support for reform had forced the resignations and returned Dubček to the forefront of Czechoslovak politics.

Dubček gestures triumphantly as if to embrace a crowd of several hundred thousand supporters in Prague, the capital city of Czechoslovakia, on November 24, 1989. Dubček had been absent from Czechoslovak politics since 1968, when his reform movement was quashed by the Soviets.

In 1968, Dubček, a loyal Communist, set out to reform the Communist dictatorship in Czechoslovakia. He wanted, he said at the time, to give socialism a "human face." What started out as a seemingly modest ambition, however, developed into a movement that shook the very foundation of the Communist world. Though Dubček never intended that the Communist party's leading role in Czechoslovakia be questioned, it was. The reforms he introduced from January to August 1968, the period that came to be known as Prague Spring, constituted a major challenge to the Soviet Union's stronghold on Communist governments in Eastern Europe.

Sabotaged by the Soviet Union, most of Czechoslovakia's Communist neighbors, and Dubček's political rivals, the reform movement failed. Stripped of his authority and thrown out of the Communist party, Dubček was forced into obscurity, a victim of the repressive Communist system he had boldly tried to reform.

The Czech people never expected to hear from Dubček again. But on November 24, 1989, following five days of demonstrations by hundreds of thousands of people and the resignation of the country's entire ruling body, the Politburo, Dubček was reunited with his people. The day before, he was seen on national television for the first time since 1968. Now he was addressing the demonstrators in Wenceslas Square.

For Dubček, it was a moment of triumph, a vindication of the principles he had followed when he had been the country's leader. "An old wise man said, 'If there once was light, why should there be darkness again?' " he told the cheering crowd. "Let us act in such a way as to bring the light back again."

Alexander Dubček was born in the small village of Uhrovec, in the Strazovska Mountains of western Slovakia, on November 27, 1921, only three years after Czechoslovakia emerged from the ashes of the old Austro-Hungarian Empire, which was defeated in World War I. Czechoslovakia was the dream of a Czech university professor named Tomáš Masaryk, who agitated throughout World War I for an independent Czechoslovak state modeled after the Western democracies. He visited the capitals of Western nations and Russia, aggressively lobbying political and business leaders, including U.S. president Woodrow Wilson, who eventually supported Masaryk's cause. As a result of Masaryk's efforts, Czechoslovakia became a nation on October 28, 1918.

A country of about 49,365 square miles, Czechoslovakia is situated in the heart of Europe and is completely landlocked. It is bordered by Poland, East Germany, West Germany, Austria, Hungary, and the Soviet Union. In the mid-1980s, Czechoslovakia had a population of nearly 16 million. Almost two-thirds of its citizens are Czechs; one-third are Slovaks. In the year the country was founded, there was also a sizable German minority (the Sudeten Germans) as well as Hungarians, Poles, and Gypsies. Because of Czechoslovakia's geographic location and its multicultural makeup, the history of

Tomáš Garrigue Masaryk, a professor of philosophy at the University of Prague, entered politics in 1891. During World War I, he led the way to the establishment of modern Czechoslovakia; he later became the new country's first president.

Czechoslovak peasants display festive native attire in Moravia, a region in central Czechoslovakia. Moravia was part of Austria-Hungary until the fall of the Hapsburg empire in World War I and the establishment of a Czechoslovak state in 1918.

its people has always been intertwined with events occurring outside its borders.

Dubček's parents, Stefan and Pavlina Dubček, were Slovaks. Although the Slovaks were related to the Czechs linguistically, having lived side by side with them for centuries, the two peoples were culturally quite different. For example, there was a sizable Protestant minority among the Czechs, whereas Slovaks were overwhelmingly Roman Catholic. Under the old Austro-Hungarian Empire, the Czech territories of Bohemia and Moravia were ruled from Vienna, whereas Slovakia came under Budapest's control. Vienna allowed the Czechs more freedom than Budapest allowed the Slovaks. While the Czechs experienced economic growth and industrial development, the Slovaks remained impoverished and less educated. Treated with contempt by its Hungarian rulers, Slovakia failed to industrialize and to develop culturally. Naturally, the Slovaks resented their oppressive rulers and were envious of the Czechs.

Stefan Dubček, a carpenter by trade, was one Slovak determined to improve his own circumstances as well as the lot of his people. Although from a humble background, he was a proud idealist, a believer in the possibility of a better, more just world for everyone, including Slovaks. He wanted more out of life than a meager existence in an impoverished Slovak village, and he believed he had found an answer in the new socialist ideologies of the day. As a young man, he had been attracted to social democracy, with its rallying call for the end of aristocratic privilege. In 1910, when Slovakia was still part of the Austro-Hungarian Empire, 19-year-old Stefan Dubček did what millions of Europeans in search of a better life did at that time: He went to America.

Stefan Dubček ended up in Chicago, where he found the promise of a better life to be a bitter disappointment. In the United States, immigrant laborers were often exploited, poorly treated, and badly paid, and Stefan Dubček proved to be no exception. He found work as a carpenter earning some $25 per week and was barely able to survive. In 1916, with World War I raging in Europe, he applied for and was granted U.S. citizenship. He then became politically active, joining the American Socialist party and supporting Eugene Debs, the Socialist candidate in the 1916 presidential election. The following year, the United States entered World War I, and Stefan Dubček was drafted into the army. Not wanting to fight in what he considered a war for imperial interests, he tried to run away to Mexico, but he was caught before crossing the border and arrested for evading the draft. He spent 18 months in prison.

By the time he was released, Stefan Dubček was politically even more radical than before. These political fires were fueled further when his new bride, Pavlina Kobidova, a Slovak immigrant who had come to the United States at age 15, introduced him to the writings of the German philosopher and economist Karl Marx. Central to Marx's philosophy was the idea that the world's economic inequities and injustices stemmed primarily from the exploitation

A woman receives a shoe-shine on the streets of Brno, Czechoslovakia, reflecting the class distinctions that divided Czechs and Slovaks during the 1920s and 1930s. The 19th-century German philosopher Karl Marx envisioned an end to such class distinctions, and his work naturally appealed to the young radical Communist Stefan Dubček.

of workers by factory owners, who lined their pockets with the profits they made from the toil of the working masses while paying them very little for their labor. Marx believed that the exploited workers would inevitably rise up in revolt and establish a new society, a "dictatorship of the proletariat," in which class divisions would break down, exploitation of the many by the few would cease, and wealth would be evenly distributed among all people.

Marx's writings had a profound impact on Stefan Dubček because exploitation, poverty, and frustration, central themes in Marx's philosophy, were no strangers to him. Pavlina, too, had known hardship; she had worked for substandard wages as a scullery maid for a well-to-do Chicago family. Though by the time they married the Dubčeks were not poor because Stefan was earning some $40 per week as a piano maker, life was still difficult for them.

The couple thought of returning home. Rapid change was taking place in Europe in the aftermath of World War I. In Russia, the old autocratic czarist regime was toppled, and power was ultimately seized by a small group of Marxist revolutionaries, the Bolsheviks, who soon renamed themselves Communists. And with the new independent Czechoslovak state, life back home no longer seemed as bleak as it once had when Stefan Dubček left 10 years before. In early 1921, he and Pavlina (already pregnant with her second child) and their baby son, Julius, set sail for Europe.

Although he found his homeland in better shape than when he left it, Stefan Dubček, like many Slovaks, was not entirely pleased with the new Czechoslovak government. It had promised a better life for Slovaks and Czechs, but policymakers in Prague were not working to develop the country's great material resources and human potential. The result was widespread unemployment and a stagnant economy.

Stefan Dubček's Marxist beliefs made him particularly dissatisfied with current government policies. Tomáš Masaryk, now president, was implementing a capitalist democracy in Czechoslovakia, and Dubček believed this meant only more exploitation of the masses by the property-owning class. In his view, the only country where there was a genuine move to create a pure Communist state was the Soviet Union, reconstituted from most of the old czarist Russian Empire. Consequently, the newly formed Czechoslovak Communist party adopted a platform that called for the overthrow of Masaryk's democratic government and the establishment of a Communist system based on the Soviet model.

But the new Soviet system was no model to follow. World War I, the revolution, and two years of civil war between the Communists and their opponents had ravaged the Soviet Union and depleted its resources. The Soviet people were tired, hungry, and frightened; the Soviet leaders were weak, insecure, and suspicious. They were glad to be rid of the czar and his corrupt entourage, but in many respects

In America you can have most things but you certainly can't have freedom. The only free country in the world is the Soviet Union.
—STEFAN DUBČEK
Alexander Dubček's father, writing home to Czechoslovakia during his time living in Chicago

the new regime was as oppressive as the last. For example, the czar's notorious secret police were replaced by the Bolsheviks' own, called the Cheka; all political parties, save the Communists, were banned; and the prisons were overflowing with alleged political criminals.

Stefan Dubček, along with most European Communists, was blind to the hardship endured by Soviet citizens. For him, the Soviet Union was the beacon of the future, and he longed to participate in the Soviet Union's grand revolutionary experiment, to be a builder of socialism. So when in the early 1920s the Soviet Union called for help from sympathetic foreign comrades to help rebuild the country, he responded. Together with other Communists in Czechoslovakia, he joined an organization called Interhelpo, committing himself and his young family to go to wherever in the Soviet Union his skills might be needed. Stefan became 1 of the 117 members of an Interhelpo group made up of artisans, factory workers, and farmers who planned to form a self-sufficient cooperative that would serve as a practical model for building a socialist economy. The Soviet government said Interhelpo's services would be particularly welcome in Pishpek (now Frunze), a remote city in the Kirghiz Republic, near the Chinese border.

On a rainy day in March 1925, Stefan, Pavlina, six-year-old Julius, and five-year-old Alexander boarded a train bound for the Soviet Union. Together with 105 other families — more than 300 people in all, including 80 children under the age of 10 — they began the 30-day, 4,000-mile journey to Pishpek. In addition to personal belongings, the group brought along a tractor, a truck, a steam engine, a lathe, a brick maker, a complete carpentry workshop, and 12 electric motors.

The trip to Pishpek was long and tiring. Though united by their Czechoslovak citizenship and Communist convictions, the Interhelpo group was divided in most other respects. They were Czechs, Slovaks, Germans, Hungarians, and Ukrainians, strangers suddenly traveling together in cramped and uncomfortable quarters. Only the thought that they were embarking on a venture that was part of

It was terrible. We did not have anything at all. We had to build our houses, and we had no tools. . . . The Soviet government gave us very little help.

—DONAT LANICEK
Slovak workman, on arriving with the Dubčeks at Pishpek in 1928

a grand effort to build a great new world made the trip bearable.

When the Interhelpo group finally arrived at Pishpek, they were sorely disappointed. Nobody was there to greet them, much less bring them to the modest houses they had been promised. Now in one of the most remote parts of the Soviet Union, they had no place to stay and were running out of food. The Kirghiz natives in Pishpek eyed them with some curiosity but made little attempt to help the newcomers get settled. Eventually, they found shelter in a dilapidated, abandoned barracks.

During the first year, the harships were so great that the Interhelpo group barely survived. They worked for little or no pay and struggled to overcome the area's harsh climate. Many of the children contracted malaria, and some died from it. One after another, people gave up and either returned to Czechoslovakia or moved to other Soviet villages. Stefan Dubček, however, was not one to give up. His belief in communism was so strong that he blamed human weakness rather than the Soviet system for the failure of the Interhelpo venture. In fact, the Dubčeks ended up staying in Pishpek for eight years.

Women drop off their babies at a day care nursery before going off to work on a collective farm outside Moscow. Stefan Dubček and his wife worked on such a farm as part of an Interhelpo group in the early 1920s, so baby Alexander may have spent some time at such a day care center.

The Dubček children began their formal education in Pishpek. Their teacher, a young Slovak who arrived with a second group of Interhelpo settlers in 1927, faced a thankless task: Not only were the children of various ages; they were also from diverse backgrounds and had no common language. The teacher conducted the lessons in Russian, making learning very difficult for his pupils.

In 1933, Stefan Dubček left the Interhelpo group and moved his family to Gorki, a city some 235 miles east of Moscow. He found a job in a car factory, and his children were finally enrolled in a proper school. Here Alexander, a shy, studious boy who spoke Russian like a native, excelled in his other studies as well. He adapted well to Gorki and was happy there.

Yet all around Alexander Dubček there was much unhappiness. The Dubčeks lived in the Soviet Union during some of that country's most turbulent, terrifying years. When they arrived in 1925, Vladimir Ilyich Ulyanov, known as Lenin, the first leader of the new Soviet state, had just died. His death had set in motion a scramble for top positions

In August 1936, encouraged by Joseph Stalin to rid the country of "enemies of the people," Soviet workers at a Leningrad machine shop vote to impose severe punishments on dissenters. Through a ruthless campaign, Stalin purged Soviet society of all those who were perceived as a threat to his absolute rule.

in the Communist party, and Joseph Stalin emerged as the new party leader. Stalin did away with cooperatives such as Interhelpo, which were too self-sufficient for his tastes, and in the early 1930s he instituted a collectivization policy aimed at nationalizing the country's farms. To do this, Stalin evicted peasants from their land and forced them to work on larger, state-owned farms. When his policy met with resistance, Stalin engineered a famine that killed millions of peasants.

In addition to declaring war on the Russian peasantry, Stalin set out to rid the Communist party of any potential threat to his leadership. One by one, he eliminated his political rivals, and before long even the average citizen had reason to fear for his life. Millions were arrested on the slightest suspicion and jailed or sent to Siberian labor camps, from which few returned. Often these innocent victims were tortured until they confessed to ludicrous charges and then were sent before a firing squad.

During these purges, any contact with foreigners such as the Dubčeks became dangerous for Soviet citizens, and out of fear their Russian friends no longer associated with them. As loyal Communists, the Dubčeks did not question Stalin's policies. Still, Pavlina and Julius Dubček returned to Czechoslovakia in 1936, and in 1938, Stefan and Alexander joined them.

Alexander Dubček (far right) and his brother, Julius (far left), pose with their aunts and uncles while on vacation in 1935. In 1933, the two boys enrolled in school in the Soviet city of Gorki. They were reunited with their parents in Czechoslovakia in 1938.

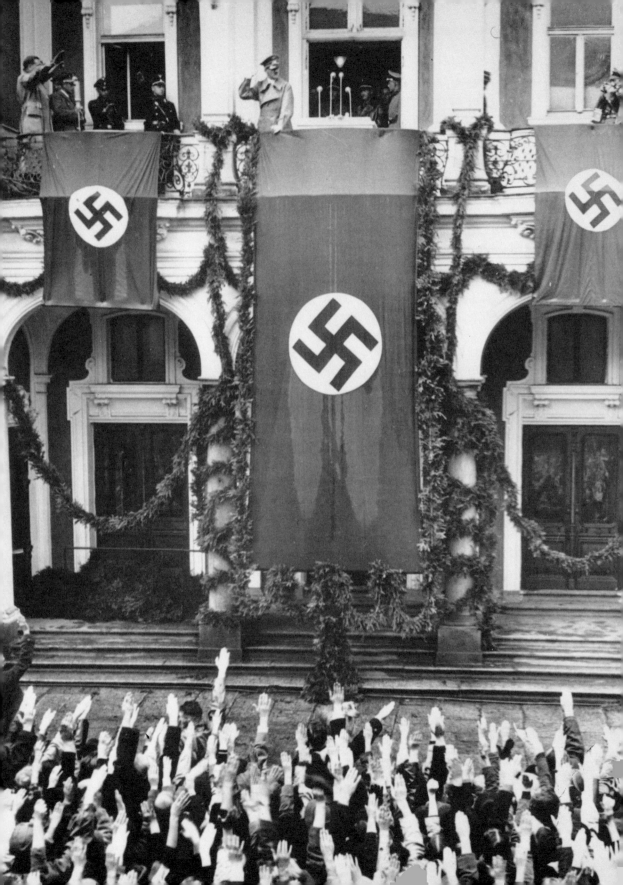

2

The Betrayal

The Dubčeks returned to Czechoslovakia on the eve of its destruction. Masaryk had retired from the presidency in 1935 and had died two years later. He was spared watching the dissolution of his dream — the independent democratic Czechoslovak state to which he had devoted his life. His successor, Edvard Beneš, was not so lucky.

The most immediate threat to Czechoslovakia was Germany. The Allied victors, particularly France, held Germany responsible for World War I and demanded that it pay reparations to the countries it had devastated. But Germany did not have the ability to meet those demands. Its most productive and industrialized region, the coal-rich Ruhr Valley, had been taken from it, and most of its resources had been depleted by the war. Then, when the Great Depression hit worldwide in the 1930s, Germany's situation became even more desperate. There was massive unemployment, a shortage of food and other goods, and consequently an extremely low morale among the German people.

Czechoslovakia [was] a country disunited, unhappy, about to be betrayed.
—WILLIAM SHAWCROSS
Dubček biographer, on Stefan and Alexander Dubček's return to Czechoslovakia in 1938

An enormous crowd of fervent Nazi supporters salute German chancellor Adolf Hitler at a mass political rally in the 1930s. Hitler came to power in 1933 bent on world domination and the annihilation of so-called inferior races.

When Adolf Hitler, leader of the National Socialist party — commonly known as the Nazis — came to power in 1933, he promised the German people that he would make Germany great again. Hitler shrewdly played on Germany's dire straits and wounded national pride. The German economy was in a shambles, and the people were desperate for jobs. They were hungry for leadership, and to many, Hitler seemed to have the wisdom and fortitude to rebuild the country. Standing before huge crowds and spouting his fanatical nationalism, Hitler, with his charisma and fiery oratory, won the admiration of the German masses.

Hitler believed that Germans, and others belonging to the so-called Aryan race, were superior to all other peoples, particularly to the Jews, whom he considered barely human. Soon after Hitler took power, he launched a virulent anti-Semitic campaign that forced German Jews out of their businesses, jobs, and homes. Ultimately, millions suffered and lost their lives in concentration camps. Hitler also considered Czechs, Slovaks, Poles, and Russians inferior peoples.

While he was conducting a systematic campaign of hate and genocide against the Jews and other "non-Aryans" and securing his position of power by exploiting the desperation of the German people, Hitler was also engaged in a plan to expand his fascist dictatorship across Europe and eventually the world. He first marched into the Ruhr Valley and reclaimed this lost territory; then, in March 1938, he marched into Austria, annexing it and meeting almost no resistance. After claiming the Lithuanian port city of Klaipeda (Memel), which had a large German population, Hitler then turned to Czechoslovakia.

At that time, Czechoslovakia also had a large German population of some 3 million people. Having never really accepted the shift in power from German-speaking Vienna in the Austro-Hungarian Empire to Czech-speaking Prague after World War I, many of Czechoslovakia's Germans stepped up their resistance throughout the 1930s. After much wrangling over a period of many months, Hitler de-

manded that Czechoslovakia cede the lands populated by these Sudeten Germans.

To that point, Czechoslovakia had met most of Hitler's demands, but to meet this latest one would have been to allow a violation of its borders, and, in effect, occupation. For support, Czechoslovakia looked to the Western democracies, particularly France, with whom it had formed a defense alliance in 1924, and also to the Soviet Union. Stalin agreed to lend a hand, but only in conjunction with a Western commitment, which was not forthcoming. France and Great Britain instead wanted to appease Hitler, in the hope that war might be averted, and set about trying to convince the Czechs and Slovaks to accept Hitler's demands.

Though abandoned by its allies, Czechoslovakia prepared to resist the impending German invasion. Meanwhile, the French and British met with Hitler in Munich in late September 1938 to decide what should become of Czechoslovakia. It was concluded that Czechoslovakia must cede all German-speaking territories to Germany within days and that all ethnic Czechs living there must leave. Within a year, Hitler marched into Prague, and a German protectorate was established in the Czech lands of Bohemia and Moravia.

British prime minister Neville Chamberlain (right) reviews German storm troopers in September 1938, when he met with Hitler to chart the future of Czechoslovakia. Chamberlain in effect gave Czechoslovakia to Hitler in an attempt to appease the German dictator's appetite for European territory.

Czech independence leader and foreign minister Edvard Beneš tips his hat for the camera as he and his wife step out of their residence in London, where they remained in exile during the Nazi occupation of Czechoslovakia.

The Munich agreement was to go down in history as one of the most shameful betrayals ever perpetrated on a nation. Dubček was not surprised by the betrayal. He had not expected France and Great Britain, countries with no immediate interest to protect in Czechoslovakia, to come to its aid. But many Czechs and Slovaks were surprised by the betrayal and now considered France and Great Britain enemies. The Soviet Union's role in the ordeal, however, strengthened its image in Czechoslovakia, and as a result, the Communist party gained popularity in Czechoslovakia throughout the war years.

With a puppet government already installed in Slovakia, Hitler looked to claim his next prize. He knew that by concluding a nonaggression pact with Stalin, he would be able to continue to expand without Soviet intervention. In the autumn of 1939, the two leaders signed such a pact, and Hitler ordered the invasion of Poland. France and Britain came to Poland's aid, but the Nazis had dug in their heels for a long, bloody fight. World War II had begun.

Alexander Dubček, now 18 years old, lost little time in rallying to the anti-Nazi cause. He had been working at odd jobs since returning from the Soviet Union — as a chauffeur, a gas station attendant, and a page boy at a local hotel. In 1939, together with Julius and Stefan, he joined the new Slovak Communist party, which was illegal under the Slovak puppet regime controlled by Hitler, a staunch anti-Communist. Soon after, he went to work as a locksmith in one of the Skoda armaments factories in Dubnica nad Vánom, close to the Slovak town of Trenčín, where the Dubček family had settled. At the factory, Dubček was involved in small-scale, but nevertheless very dangerous, clandestine activities. With the occupation of Czechoslovakia, one prize that Hitler was most pleased in obtaining was the famous Skoda armaments works. Czechoslovakia was then, and is still today, a top manufacturer of sophisticated weaponry. Hitler wanted the Skoda works for his war effort, and he got it. Dubček's job, as part of a small, tightly knit Communist cell in his factory, was to sabotage production and steal as much equipment as possible. As the armaments factories were particularly well guarded by the secret police, this was no task for the careless or the sloppy: Detection could cost one's life.

Two Czech women give the Nazi salute during the German occupation of their country. With occupying forces and a puppet government firmly established in Prague, Hitler invaded Poland in the autumn of 1939, hoping to expand his empire further.

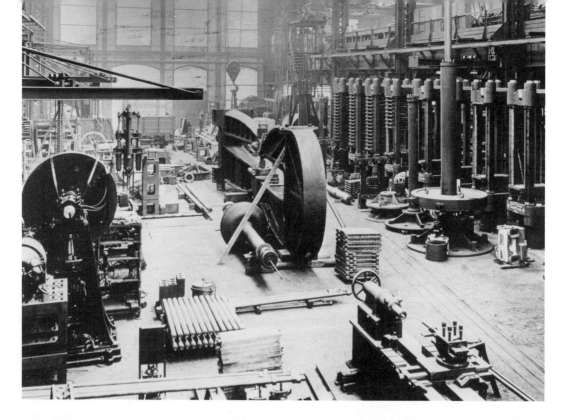

The Skoda armaments factory, near Trenčín, where Dubček worked as a locksmith in 1939. While there, Dubček engaged in clandestine, pro-Communist activities in an effort to foil the Nazis.

Up until 1939, there had been only one Communist party in Czechoslovakia — the Czech one. It had a Slovak section, which was considered subordinate to Prague. Now, with the country split, the Slovaks formed their own independent Communist party. It was in this newly created Slovak party that Dubček met many of the men who would be his comrades-in-arms, his political colleagues, his supporters, and his detractors in the years ahead. During the war, Dubček was still an insignificant, inconspicuous cadre, whereas many of his later colleagues in the party were already distinguished leaders. The relationship these Communists would have with one another in the future would sometimes be contradictory and confusing. Their individual destinies in Czechoslovakia started out on one kind of path and ended up on another. Frequently, party members would be denounced by their closest colleagues or embraced by their most bitter foes, blurring the distinction between friend and enemy. This unpredictability among party members made it seem as though the strings were being pulled by an invisible hand, setting opposing forces in motion.

In a very real sense, that is exactly what was going on. The string puller was Joseph Stalin, although the Czech and Slovak Communists were largely unaware of this at the time. Stalin wanted to control all Communist activity, both at home and abroad. One way to do this was to have Moscow-trained Communists in leading party roles. This is what he sought to accomplish in Czechoslovakia.

Many Communists in Czechoslovakia — mostly from the Czech party — either found themselves in prison soon after the Nazis took over or, like party leader Klement Gottwald, fled to Moscow. The Czech party was thus hampered in its activities. The vacuum it left was soon filled by the Slovak Communist party. It was still separate from the Czech party and, being new, still somewhat outside the sphere of Stalin's influence. It included men such as Vladimír (Vlado) Clementis and Gustav Husák.

During World War II, Husák joined forces with democratic elements in Slovakia in resisting the Nazi occupation. This strategy did not please Stalin, but it proved highly effective for Communists in the country, as they became more and more identified with the effort to defend Czechoslovakia against the Germans. As a result, the Slovak party began to train cadres for guerrilla warfare and planned a general revolt against the Nazis. Both Alexander and Julius Dubček were part of this effort.

Stefan Dubček, however, was not. He was arrested for his political activities in 1943 and spent two years in jail in Slovakia. Once, he made plans to escape and revealed those plans to another Slovak Communist jailed with him, Viliam Siroky. When Siroky betrayed Stefan Dubček to the prison officials, the escape plan was abandoned. Siroky later succeeded in escaping himself, whereas in February 1945, Stefan Dubček was transported to the Nazi concentration camp of Mauthausen. Perhaps because there were only a few months left to the war, he survived the ordeal. Years of imprisonment had a profound effect on Stefan Dubček and changed his life in very personal and unexpected ways. During a second failed escape attempt he was hidden for a number of days by a peasant woman living on

In a cartoon from a World War II underground Czechoslovak paper, Nazi-occupied Czechoslovakia is depicted as a prison supported only by the shaky pillars of (left to right) murder, violence, robbery, treason, lies, and corruption.

the Austrian border. After the war, he divorced Pavlina and married this woman. It is unknown if Stefan's decision to divorce and remarry strained his relationship with his sons. It is clear, however, that by the time Alexander became Czechoslovakia's leader, he was very close to both his parents.

While Stefan Dubček was in prison, Alexander and Julius took part in the Slovak revolt, joining the Jan Ziska Brigade, made up of 500 men. In the fall of 1944, there were at least nine such brigades, and they prepared for a general uprising against the Nazis in late August 1944. Although the war had turned against Hitler long before and was almost over, the Nazi occupation of Czechoslovakia was brutal up until the final days. The revolt was swiftly and decisively put down. Extra forces from Germany's secret police, the Gestapo, flooded Slovakia. Suspected partisans were killed, as were countless civilians. One morning, the workers in Alexander's armaments factory were confronted by the corpses of five former employees who had been hanged the day before on charges of sabotage. The warning was clear.

Alexander had luckily concealed his clandestine role when on the job. But the Dubček family was not to emerge from World War II unscathed. Fun-loving, easygoing Julius, the very opposite of his serious younger brother, was shot and killed by a German patrol one night in January 1945, just shortly before Stefan was sent to Mauthausen. In another incident, Alexander was shot twice in the thigh and had to be carried on a stretcher to a local house, where he was nursed back to health by his mother and his future wife. Alexander Dubček's days as an active partisan were thus cut short.

The Slovak revolt did not succeed in routing the Nazis. Nor did it pave the way, as its leaders had hoped, for the Soviet Red Army to cross Slovakia unhindered. But it provided the Slovak Communist party with a certain glory that it would need in the postwar years, when its authority would come under severe attack from Czech Communists, and it had the short-term effect of harassing the Nazis.

> *During the worst trials a man of courage and honesty, a fighter for the new Czechoslovak Republic and for the interests of its working people. He was an exemplary, modest and self-sacrificing Communist.*
>
> —description by comrades-in-arms of Dubček's war service with the partisans, 1944

Wenceslas Square, Prague, in the aftermath of World War II. Following the war, Czechoslovakia began a period of restoration: Beneš was elected president in 1946, and a modified republican government was instituted.

The revolt also helped Beneš, who had formed a government-in-exile in London in 1942, convince Western powers that Slovakia was not an enemy state (Hitler's local puppet regime notwithstanding) and should be included with the Czech lands in reestablishing a single country after the war.

Despite the Slovak revolt's military defeat, the Red Army defeated the Germans on the eastern front. At the same time, the American army liberated parts of western Czechoslovakia. These were the final days of World War II. Once again, Germany would be utterly defeated.

The war ended in Europe on May 7, 1945. Days earlier, Hitler had committed suicide beneath the bombed-out streets of Berlin. Europe lay in ruins. With an estimated 45 million people dead, World War II had been the costliest war in human history. Western Europe began to rebuild. But for Czechoslovakia — with 360,000 of its people dead and another 2 million reduced to slavery by the Nazis — and other East European countries, rebuilding would take much longer. A new kind of struggle was about to begin.

3

The Loyal Apparatchik

Plans for how the postwar map of Europe would be redrawn were already well under way even while Hitler was still exhorting the children of Berlin to fight until the last one fell. The leaders of the Allied powers — Prime Minister Winston Churchill of Great Britain, U.S. president Franklin Roosevelt, and the Soviet Union's Joseph Stalin — met in Yalta in the Soviet Crimea in February 1945 to decide the future of Europe.

When the Allied leaders conferred at Yalta, the Soviet army had already liberated Romania, Bulgaria, Yugoslavia, and Poland from the Germans and had already entered Hungary, Czechoslovakia, and even Germany itself. Nearly 7 million Soviet soldiers were in Eastern Europe, some of them a mere 40 miles from Berlin. This certainly helped Stalin's negotiating position.

Given the Soviet Union's contribution to the Allied victory over the Germans and its enormous losses — some 20 million dead — Roosevelt and Churchill accepted Stalin's claims that he had a right to a buffer zone in Eastern Europe. But the Western

The man Dubček is remarkable for his innocent honesty. He may well reach the top of the Party—but he is more likely to find himself in prison.
—Slovakian Communist journalist, writing during the purges

On February 25, 1948, a massive crowd in Wenceslas Square cheers upon hearing an announcement that a third Czechoslovak republic would be formed. The elation was short-lived, however, as the hard-line Communists seized power within days.

The "Big Three" — British prime minister Winston Churchill, U.S. president Franklin D. Roosevelt, and Soviet leader Joseph Stalin — meet at Yalta, in the Soviet Union, to decide the geopolitical fate of postwar Europe.

leaders wanted assurances that in all the countries liberated by the Red Army, people would be free to decide their own future. So Stalin promised to hold free elections. But he had no intention of allowing these elections to take place: Stalin wanted complete control over Eastern Europe.

Stalin's method of securing control, however, was not all that obvious at first. Communists in each of the Eastern European countries under the Soviet sphere of influence — Albania, Yugoslavia, Bulgaria, Romania, Poland, Hungary, Czechoslovakia, and East Germany — were instructed to form broad coalitions with other parties, including non-Communists who had been in opposition to the ousted German Nazis or their locally installed Fascist regimes. The Communists were to support broad social reforms and democratic initiatives designed to give people more say in public life. The strategy was to gain popularity while at the same time consolidating power. The Communists were then to eliminate their non-Communist coalition partners — quietly at first — from any government office or influential position. When strong enough, the Communist party was to take over completely. If possible, this would be done with Moscow-trained cadres, loyal to Stalin, in leading roles.

In less than a year, Stalin's plan was a success. By the time Western leaders realized Stalin's true intentions, it was too late. In March 1946, Winston Churchill admitted that an "iron curtain" had now descended on that part of Europe that stretched from the Baltic to the Adriatic seas.

The wartime Western alliance with the Soviet Union disintegrated into a bitter conflict that stopped just short of open warfare — a cold war — as Europe found itself politically and ideologically divided. The Soviet Union had emerged as a world superpower with a belligerent attitude toward its counterpart, the United States. A race to produce armaments — including nuclear weapons — began on both sides. The two superpowers also consolidated the military defenses of their respective spheres of influence. The United States, along with most countries of Western Europe, formed the North Atlantic Treaty Organization (NATO) in 1949 to coordinate their joint defense strategies. In 1955, with the same purpose in mind, the Eastern European countries formed the Warsaw Treaty Organization, commonly known as the Warsaw Pact. It would be 40 years before relations between the superpowers — and consequently, the fate of Eastern Europe — would substantially improve. During that time, Czechoslovakia had extremely limited options about how to shape its own future.

In the immediate postwar years, the coalition formed between Communists and their democratic non-Communist partners was slightly different in Czechoslovakia than elsewhere. Here the Communists didn't have to face a sullen and resentful population, as, for example, they did in Poland. In free, unhampered elections in 1946, the Communist party won more than 38 percent of the vote, proof that the Czechoslovak nation did not forget that the Soviets had been there in the fight against the Nazi occupation. In part, the Communists also won because they had initiated a land distribution scheme whereby poor peasants were given land that had been appropriated from the Sudeten Germans, who were kicked out of their homes after the war, much as the Czechs had been dispossessed by Hitler. Some 3 million Germans were deported. Czech peasants, gleeful that there were such tangible benefits to revenge, were unaware that as soon as they came to power, the Communists intended to take the land away again to implement Soviet-style collectivization.

The coalition government from 1945 to 1948, called the National Front, derived some legitimacy from the fact that President Beneš had returned from exile to be its leader. And Beneš was quite willing to share power with the Communists: Klement Gottwald, head of the Czech Communist party, became premier in 1946.

From the beginning, though, Stalin's plan was carefully being orchestrated. Communists were appointed heads of 12 ministries, including such key ones as Defense, Interior, Information, Finance, and Agriculture. There were still 11 non-Communist ministers, including Jan Masaryk, son of Czechoslovakia's first president, Tomáš Masaryk. He headed the important and prestigious Foreign Ministry. In the following two years, friction inevitably resulted as the Czechoslovak Communists were pressured from Moscow to put the interests of the Soviet Union above those of their own country. Thus, while Western Europe was rapidly rebuilding its ravaged cities as a result of the United States's European Recovery Program, Czechoslovakia had to stand helplessly by and watch. Though many, including some Communists, wanted to accept the offer of U.S. aid, Stalin said no. He didn't want the West to have any leverage in his buffer zone.

Beneš had already experienced Stalin's heavy hand on the issue of Transcarpathia, an ethnically mixed area that was part of eastern Czechoslovakia. Stalin had promised Beneš in 1943 that the region, overrun by Germany, would be returned to Czechoslovakia after the war. He did not keep his promise.

> *A great milestone in our development.*
> —ALEXANDER DUBČEK
> endorsing the Communist
> takeover of power in
> February 1948

Instead, Transcarpathia was incorporated into the Soviet Union.

During the first days after the war, Alexander Dubček was concerned with more elemental questions. He was 24 years old, and except for his experience as a locksmith, he had few other skills. Along with millions of other unemployed, unskilled laborers, Dubček went looking for a job.

When he came home to Trenčín, Dubček quickly found a job at a local yeast factory. He also became involved in the activities of the local Communist party and was soon appointed party secretary at his factory. His duties for this unpaid job — which he performed in his spare time — included recruiting new members, organizing meetings, and collecting dues. He was also to instruct other Communists in the factory on whatever directives higher party officials wanted the workers to follow, be these strikes or walkouts or negotiations with the factory management.

So began Dubček's life as a Communist party member in peacetime. Gone were clandestine activities conducted under the threat of death; gone were the days of partisan warfare. Until he suddenly appeared on the national scene in Czechoslovakia in 1968, Dubček's career would be made up of a stream of such steady steps up the party hierarchy. Dubček was to become part of the impersonal Communist bureaucracy that grew ever more alien from the people it purported to serve. Despite being a part of this bureaucracy, Dubček managed to survive Czechoslovakia's bleakest postwar days with both his integrity — at least most of it — and his party loyalty intact.

In 1968, Dubček was probably the only Communist leader in Eastern Europe who had been married in a Roman Catholic church. In November 1945, he married a local Slovak woman, Anna Ondrisova, whom he had first met in the Soviet Union when both their families were members of the Interhelpo group. Anna had returned to Czechoslovakia in the early 1930s. Later, during Alexander's partisan days, she had nursed him as he convalesced from his wounds. It was Anna who wanted to be married

In November 1945, Dubček married Anna Ondrisova, a Slovak woman whom he had met in the Soviet Union. Though Dubček had no religious convictions, he honored Anna's wish that they be married in a church.

Gustav Husák (left), future chairman of the Czechoslovak Communist party, and Czechoslovak president Klement Gottwald in 1948. By the end of that year, despite the efforts of Beneš, Gottwald and the Communists had begun a process of Sovietization in Czechoslovakia.

in a church, and Alexander agreed to it. The priest who married the couple had been a fellow partisan and during the war had brought the wounded Alexander to Anna's house.

Czechoslovakia's uneasy coalition days were numbered. As Communists and non-Communists pursued contradictory policies, tension mounted. Communists began packing the police force with their own members. In 1948, as another election was coming up, non-Communists protested and demanded that the situation be corrected. The Communist minister in charge of the police refused to appoint non-Communists, even when President Beneš ordered him to comply with the demand. In February 1948, the 11 non-Communist ministers resigned, believing that this would force the Communist ministers — and Premier Gottwald — to do so as well. Instead, Communists seized the vacant posts, filling them with party members. Reluctantly,

President Beneš was forced to acknowledge these new officials. Non-Communist leaders began to flee the country. Jan Masaryk, however, vacillated and paid for the missed opportunity with his life. On March 10, 1948, he plunged to his death from an office window at the Foreign Ministry. The official Communist explanation was that Masaryk jumped; the unofficial non-Communist one was that he was pushed.

Gottwald then embarked on an unprecedented recruitment drive for the party. By November 1948, membership had doubled to 2.5 million people, some 18 percent of the population and almost 1 out of every 3 Czechoslovak adults. Only the Soviet Communist party had more members. A new, Soviet-style constitution, which declared Czechoslovakia a "people's democracy," was ratified by the Constituent Assembly in May 1948. It retained some democratic features from the constitution used since 1918 but for the most part ensured Communist control. Beneš refused to ratify the new constitution, resigned, and died three months later.

On March 10, 1948, Jan Masaryk, the Czechoslovak foreign minister and the son of Czechoslovakia's first president, fell to his death from a window at the Foreign Ministry. The incident was officially called a suicide, but many suspected foul play on the part of the government.

Under large portraits of Joseph Stalin and Klement Gottwald, a local committee signs a five-year collectivization agreement in Brno, Czechoslovakia. In similar ceremonies throughout Czechoslovakia, private farms and industries were turned over to the state.

The Sovietization of Czechoslovakia began in earnest. All industry was nationalized. Land was confiscated from the peasants, collective farms were established, and businessmen lost their companies as all such assets were turned over to the state. Anyone who actively opposed the new measures was classified as an "enemy of the people" and imprisoned.

The political and economic repercussions of these measures for Czechoslovakia's people were devastating. Thousands fled the country. Others, especially non-Communist politicians, were arrested on charges of treason, and many were executed. Czechoslovakia's democratic traditions were being mercilessly trampled on and eradicated.

As a young cadre with a limited perspective, Alexander Dubček was unaware of the full scale of the repression. He was pleased that the Communists had finally come to full power in Czechoslovakia. He hoped that now perhaps the most just of all states — the Communist one, where there would be no reactionary nationalists and no privileged classes exploiting workers — would emerge in his own homeland.

It is difficult to understand how Dubček could remain loyal to the Communists when so many innocent people all around him were suffering at the hands of the system. Members of his own family suffered. For example, his uncle Michael — Stefan's brother — had built up a modest business as a tailor, representing more than 20 years of his lifework. When the business was taken away from him by the Communist-led nationalization drive, the distraught man threw himself in front of a speeding train. It is not known how Dubček dealt personally with the tragedy of his uncle's death, but it does not seem to have shaken his belief in communism.

In 1949, Dubček left his job at the yeast factory to become part of the Communist bureaucracy — colloquially known in Eastern Europe and the Soviet Union as "the apparat." Dubček was now a full-time bureaucrat, an apparatchik. His job as one of Trenčín's 15 local party secretaries was to help implement the nationalization of the land and small businesses, in other words to confiscate people's property and assets on party orders. Attending to his job with firm dedication, Dubček became a willing instrument in what was basically unfair and indecent discrimination.

Dubček was rewarded for his loyalty and service to the party; he soon began moving up the apparat ladder. In 1951, he became a bureaucrat in the Central Committee headquarters of the Slovak Communist party in Bratislava, the region's capital. He was also elected to the Legislative Assembly. This forum still maintained a parliamentary structure but no longer worked as one. Along with the rest of the government, the Legislative Assembly was by now just a rubber stamp for the Communist party.

Thus, Dubček was already a well-entrenched, albeit minor, apparatchik when Stalin pulled the strings of his puppets one last time, unleashing a terror unmatched since the 1930s purges of the Communist party in the Soviet Union. Once again, the terror would begin in Moscow. Only this time it would be duplicated in the unsuspecting and unprepared satellite countries of Eastern Europe. And, as in the 1930s, Alexander Dubček would remain oblivious to most of what would happen.

Unrealistic targets of Communist planning, forced collectivization of agriculture, growing dependence of the country's economy on the Soviet Union—all resulted in an economic crisis of unprecedented gravity.
—Czechoslovak commentator, in 1952, on the failure of the economic propaganda campaigns to improve living conditions after the war

4

The Puppets Dance

When Joseph Stalin turned 70 years old in 1949, he was probably the most powerful man on earth. Not only was he dictator of what was geographically the largest country in the world, he was also now the de facto emperor of Eastern Europe. Czechoslovakia, like the rest of the satellite countries, was rapidly becoming a miniature replica of the Soviet Union's totalitarian system. Because Stalin controlled everything, the decisions he made had a direct and often tragic impact on millions of people in Eastern Europe as well as at home.

Stalin was in failing health, and the paranoia central to his character throughout his life now became more pronounced than ever. He saw plots and conspirators everywhere, from his own inner circle of sycophantic lieutenants to the Communist leaders of the Eastern European countries. As in the 1930s, he decided to rid himself of these imagined traitors and began laying the groundwork for a new round of purges.

He was methodical, all embracing, and total as a criminal. He was one of those rare terrible dogmatists capable of destroying nine-tenths of the human race to make happy the one-tenth.
—MILOVAN DJILAS
member of the Yugoslav Politburo, on Joseph Stalin

Soviet leader Joseph Stalin (left) appears at a rally with Vyacheslav Molotov, the Soviet Union's commissar for foreign affairs. By purging the government of all opposition, Stalin remained in power in the Soviet Union for more than a quarter century.

Yugoslav premier Josip Broz Tito (wearing white shoes) chats with delegates to the Fifth Congress of the Communist party of Yugoslavia. Like Dubček, Tito was a devout Communist with a strong belief in the need for political, economic, and social reform.

Those who had survived the previous terror knew there was something ominous in the air when Stalin began making speeches calling for new blood in the party. The current party cadres had grown too lazy, too complacent, he complained. Room had to be made for younger, more energetic members. These were the kinds of speeches Stalin had made right before hundreds of thousands of people were arrested on trumped-up charges in the 1930s. If Stalin said that new blood was needed, it probably meant that old blood would soon be spilled.

But Stalin had never operated directly in eliminating his enemies. He set his traps carefully. When they were sprung, the unsuspecting victims often didn't realize what had happened to them. Stalin characterized the "guilty" as those who had engaged in spying for Western intelligence agencies, who had exhibited bourgeois nationalist sentiments, and who had shown signs of cosmopolitanism. In doing so, Stalin played on the latent prejudices, the rigid party discipline that never questioned authority, and the terror-induced psychology of those who would actually carry out his plans. In Czechoslovakia, Stalin's methods would have tragic consequences.

Stalin interpreted the phrase "spying for Western intelligence agencies" somewhat loosely. It came to apply to anyone who had either been in the West or had contact with Westerners. Among Eastern European Communist leaders, there were many who in the mid-1930s had fought in the Spanish civil war against the Fascist forces of Francisco Franco. Although they had done so out of their Communist convictions, now such participation was enough to cast suspicion on them. These men had, of course, come into contact with like-minded Western fighters. It took a great leap of the imagination to interpret such contacts as conspiring to spy for Western intelligence agencies, but Stalin made the leap. The first part of the trap was set.

Next, Stalin turned against those Communists who had not been trained in Moscow. Their loyalty to him, he suspected, was questionable. In 1948, Stalin's authority was faced with its greatest challenge from Josip Broz Tito, Yugoslavia's Communist leader. While Tito considered himself as much a Communist as Joseph Stalin, he refused to put the interests of the Soviet Union above those of Yugoslavia — and said so. Because Tito had been in charge of a large partisan army in Yugoslavia during the war, he had the popular backing of his people, and Stalin could do little to displace him. So he banished Tito from the Soviet camp, denouncing him as a traitor. But the Soviet dictator had to make sure that no one else in Eastern Europe was tempted to follow Tito's example. He went after other "home Communists," such as Gustav Husák, who, paying little attention to whether Stalin approved, had directed Communist activities in Slovakia during the war. Husák was now denounced as "a bourgeois nationalist"; and many other top leaders of the Slovak Communist party were condemned along with him for the same alleged sin. Dubček, luckily, was at this time too unimportant to be caught in the dragnet. He quietly kept on working at the Slovak Central Committee's offices in Bratislava while this second trap was set.

Lastly, the derogatory term "cosmopolitanism" was a thinly veiled attack on Jews. Cosmopolitans,

Gustav Husák speaks at a workers' rally in 1946. In April 1954, Husák, a Slovak, was tried and sentenced to life imprisonment for being a "bourgeois nationalist," a Soviet term for someone whose loyalty to the party has been compromised by nationalist sentiment. He was released in 1960.

Rudolf Slánský, general secretary of the Czechoslovak Communist party, was arrested, tried, and executed for crimes he never committed. Though wrongly convicted, Slánský was one of Stalin's closest colleagues during the purges of the 1930s and was thus guilty of many horrible crimes for which he was never tried.

according to Stalin, had loyalties superseding those to the country in which they were born, and if they were Communists, to the party to which they belonged. Stalin's anti-Semitism in the late 1940s became more virulent. Many of his Jewish victims had been dedicated believers in the ideals of communism. A few, such as the general secretary of the Czech Communist party, Rudolf Slánský, had been guilty of many things, but disloyalty and the other charges cooked up by Stalin were not among them. Ironically, Slánský initiated Stalin's terror in Czechoslovakia; he was responsible for the first wave of arrests and had favored setting up labor camps for political prisoners.

The traps were now set, the crimes defined. All that remained was to conjure up the criminals.

Stalin's henchmen fanned out all over Eastern Europe to uncover the "enemies of the people." In Czechoslovakia, they formed a parallel group working in cooperation with select members of the Czech secret police. Hundreds of Communists and non-Communists alike were arrested. Although Stalin had particular levels of officialdom in mind as his victims, they were by no means the only ones who suffered. The purges also constituted a wide-scale effort to terrorize the Czechoslovak population into submission. Everyone was either affected personally or knew someone who was. Religious leaders, non-Communist politicians, shopkeepers, teachers, students, writers, and many others were imprisoned. Anyone who belonged to the wrong class was suspect. Anyone who had a house, some land, or other possessions that a local party boss wanted could end up in prison.

Not only people but ideas, too, were purged. Some 7 million books were confiscated by the authorities from private collections and kept under lock and key. Another 7 million were destroyed. History was "revised" so that men such as Tomáš Masaryk and Edvard Beneš were made out to be traitors.

In the prisons, after brutal interrogations, threats, and torture, scores of people were forced to "confess" to conspiratorial crimes. Thus, a conspiracy of major proportions among the Czechoslovak leadership was fabricated. In the most notorious of the trials, the noose tightened around the neck of top Communist party officials who were Jews. Men such as the respected Vlado Clementis, who had succeeded Jan Masaryk as foreign minister; the dedicated Rudolf Margolius, deputy minister of foreign trade; and 12 others were arrested on trumped-up charges of conspiracy. Rudolf Slánský, given his complete obedience to Stalin, was at first an unlikely target. Yet none of the others held important enough positions to be considered the ringleader of the fictitious conspiracy. As general secretary of the Czechoslovak Communist party, Slánský did. Being a Jew sealed his fate.

Under severe torture, the accused men all confessed to outrageous charges. Newspapers were filled with made-up details of how they had betrayed communism. Their wives and children were ostracized and pressured to denounce them, which some did. One 16-year-old boy wrote a letter to *Rude Pravo*, the Czech Communist party newspaper, calling for the death sentence for the traitor who was his father. As Heda Margolius, wife of Rudolf Margolius, later sadly commented, "It is harder to say

Vladimír Clementis succeeded Jan Masaryk at the Foreign Ministry following the latter's alleged suicide. Like Husák, Clementis, in 1951, was charged with bourgeois nationalism. However, Husák was merely jailed for his alleged crimes, whereas Clementis was executed.

Eight people convicted on trumped-up charges of treason and other crimes against the state and the Communist party await their dire fate. Some 120,000 people were arrested, executed, or sentenced to prison during the Soviet purges in Czechoslovakia during the late 1940s and 1950s.

whose fate was more tragic, that of the father who went to his death accompanied by those words or that of the son who would have to go through life with the memory of having written them."

Eleven of the Slánský trial defendants were executed. Three were given sentences of life imprisonment. One of these men, Eduard Goldstuecker, would emerge in 1968 as part of Dubček's reform movement. In fact, the push for reforms would come from many of the Communist purge victims.

In all, the purges claimed the lives of some 180 of the country's politicians. Many more died who were not Communist party members, and still other party members were imprisoned. In 1968, when the full extent of the purges was revealed for the first time, it was estimated that between 120,000 and 140,000 people had either been arrested, executed, or sentenced to prison terms or forced labor.

Alexander Dubček was in Bratislava when the purges were at their height, as one by one several of the Slovak party's key members disappeared. Gustav Husák, for example, was thrown out of the party in 1950 and four years later was tried and sentenced to life imprisonment. Part of Dubček's job was to pass on party directives from Prague to the smaller regions and districts, so he was always well informed of inside developments. But, as he had in the Soviet Union, Dubček failed to guess what was really behind all the purges. Rather, he was usually inclined to believe what the party said — unless he himself had direct knowledge from his own personal experience.

In 1952, Dubček showed that he was unafraid of going against the prevailing dogma when he spoke at the funeral of an old and committed Slovak Communist, Karol Smidke. Smidke had been one of those Slovaks thrown out of the party for "bourgeois nationalism." He was shunned by everyone. When he died, only Dubček and a handful of people attended the funeral. By delivering a sincere and heartfelt eulogy, Dubček demonstrated that for him simple humanity superseded political discipline.

Though no one actually suffered at the hands of Dubček during the purges, he did not emerge entirely unsullied. In the early 1950s, for example, he publicly denounced Rudolf Slánský in a speech. This was mild compared to what others were saying at the time, and Dubček's tone had none of the hysteria of several of his colleagues. Still, it was not one of his finest moments.

On March 5, 1953, Joseph Stalin lost the ultimate power play — the one with death. His successors drew a breath of relief, resolved that in the future the leadership would be collective, and then prepared themselves for the infighting that would determine who was really to inherit Stalin's crown.

Although Stalin had determined the policies, the actual dirty work in each Eastern European country had been done by local leaders. In Czechoslovakia, Klement Gottwald had been manipulated into betraying Slánský, who had been his close associate for more than 20 years. These betrayals were perpetrated throughout the Communist party structure and society in general. Although at first unwitting accomplices, Czechoslovakia's Communist rulers now shared the guilt. Long after Stalin died, it was not politic to speak about the enormous injustices he had perpetrated, and this silence, which no one was brave enough to break, would last well into the next decade.

> *A man who was in prison may get back his freedom, the accusations against him may be retracted, he may even get back his citizens' rights and obtain financial indemnity, but no one can indemnify him for the loss of human dignity that he suffered.*
> —EDUARD GOLDSTUECKER
> Communist leader deposed during the purges

5

Climbing the Party Ladder

After Stalin's death, the reshuffling of power in the Kremlin was quickly followed by a similar reshuffling in Prague. Just days after Stalin's funeral, Klement Gottwald died, and a new hierarchy was established in Czechoslovakia. Antonín Zápotocký succeeded Gottwald, and Stefan Dubček's onetime fellow prisoner, Viliam Siroky, became premier. Antonín Novotný, the Communist capo from the elder Dubček's concentration camp days, had already taken over Rudolf Slánský's post of general secretary of the Czechoslovak Communist party.

Alexander Dubček was promoted: He became regional party secretary of Banská Bystrica, a town framed by the lower Tatry Mountains in central Slovakia. Dubček was pleased that this new job would bring him into contact with ordinary people again. He was responsible for developing the economic resources of his area and implementing government policies. For two years, Dubček presided over the partial industrialization of the town's economy.

The unity of the socialist camp is the guarantee of our progress; faithful to the principles of proletarian internationalism we shall guard this unity as the basic condition of the full and final victory over defunct capitalism.
—ALEXANDER DUBČEK

Dubček and his three sons — Milan, Pavel, and Peter — at home in Bratislava in 1957. Though perpetually occupied with complex affairs of government, Dubček, a devoted family man, always found time to spend with his children while they were growing up.

Soviet leader Nikita Khrushchev waves to a Prague crowd during a visit to Czechoslovakia in July 1957. The year before, during a closed session of the 20th Party Congress, Khrushchev had strengthened his own position by revealing the truth about the atrocities of the Stalin era and thereby linking his political rivals with those crimes.

During his tenure, four large new factories were built — a lumber mill, a textile factory, a pharmaceutical laboratory, and a cement works. In addition, he continued the Soviet-style collectivization policies being enforced throughout the country. As in the rest of Slovakia, Banská Bystrica's economy was primarily agricultural. By the time Dubček arrived, more than 40 percent of the farms had been collectivized in a 5-year period. The peasants' resistance to giving up their privately owned farms was still strong, however, and Dubček faced a considerable challenge in implementing this policy.

Despite the political turmoil in Czechoslovakia, the 1950s were years of great personal happiness for Alexander Dubček. Now the father of three young sons, Peter, Pavel, and Milan, Dubček was a devoted family man who spent his free hours with his children, his wife, or his parents. On weekends, Dubček worked in his garden or took his sons to a soccer game. The family frequently enjoyed hiking together

in the forest or swimming at the municipal swimming pool.

Unlike so many of his colleagues, Dubček enjoyed a simple life, never using his position to secure lavish material privileges for himself. He was never seen in the special vacation resorts reserved for high party officials, and he did not move his family into the special compounds where only party officials were allowed to live. In Bratislava, the Dubček family rented a modest one-family house. In Banská Bystrica, their new home was similarly unassuming.

While at Banská Bystrica, Dubček began to study law at night, and he was eventually awarded a degree from Comenius University in Bratislava. Then, in 1955, he was chosen by the Slovak Communist party to attend Moscow's prestigious Higher Party School, where he enrolled in a three-year program. The curriculum emphasized the study of Communist ideology, particularly the writings of Marx, Marx's associate Friedrich Engels, and Lenin.

A bust of Stalin is vandalized in Budapest, Hungary, in 1956. That year, Khrushchev's speech triggered a de-Stalinization movement in the Soviet Union and sent shock waves throughout Eastern Europe, where de-Stalinization meant de-Sovietization.

While in Moscow, Dubček learned a great deal by observing the dramatic political developments taking place there. In 1956, at the 20th Party Congress, a party official from the Ukraine, Nikita Khrushchev, delivered a secret speech in which he formally denounced Stalin and for several hours read aloud a partial list of the dead dictator's crimes. With this bold move, Khrushchev succeeded in linking his political rivals to Stalin's terror, thereby hindering their chances for success. Soon Khrushchev emerged the undisputed victor in the Kremlin power struggle and became head of the Soviet Communist party.

As a result of Khrushchev's revelations, millions of people in the Soviet Union who had been dishonored by Stalin were allowed to resume a more normal life. The gates of labor camps in Siberia were opened, and some 8 million political prisoners were released. Some were rehabilitated — that is, cleared of the charges made against them — and some even resumed their former jobs. Also, culture and the arts flourished, as writers and poets began to experiment and publish their work more openly. In addition, public opinion became an important political force in the Soviet Union.

Khrushchev never anticipated the effect that the revelation of Stalin's crimes would have on the Eastern European satellite states, where de-Stalinization was interpreted as getting rid of Soviet power. Riots broke out in Poland, and a full-scale uprising, supported by Communist leader Imre Nagy, erupted in Hungary. Nagy not only wanted to get rid of his own Hungarian Stalinists but wanted also to withdraw Hungary from the Warsaw Pact. This Khrushchev would not tolerate, and tanks were sent in to crush the 1956 rebellion. Nagy, along with hundreds of other Hungarian reformers, was arrested and executed.

Graduated with honors from the Higher Party School, Dubček returned to Czechoslovakia with a doctorate in political science. His three years in Moscow had given him a perspective by which to judge his own colleagues and superiors in the Czechoslovak party when he returned. Before, he had loyally administered policies set by his superiors, trusting that they were formulated with the best interests of the party and the people in mind. Now Dubček realized that many party bosses acted out of less than noble motives. With this newly acquired political savvy, the seeds of Dubček's eventual nonconformity were planted.

Still, it would take another decade before those seeds flowered. When Dubček returned to Czechoslovakia in 1958, little had changed. Unlike neighboring Hungary or Poland, Czechoslovakia had not experienced the shock waves of de-Stalinization. By the mid-1950s, the purge trials themselves had stopped, and a few people had been quietly released from prison. But many more remained. In a few token gestures, some minor officials who had been implicated in the purges were removed from office,

We shall absolutely refuse to permit anyone to misuse matters which have been solved long ago for demogogical attacks against the Party.
—ANTONIN NOVOTNÝ
Czechoslovak Communist leader, defying demands to investigate the crimes of the Stalin era

but those guilty of major complicity were still in power. In fact, Antonín Novotný, who had been instrumental in the purges, had gained even more power than he had before: In 1957, Zápotocký died, and Novotný took over his post as president while also retaining the position of the Czechoslovak party leader.

Novotný disliked Dubček, and relations between the two men worsened as Dubček moved up the party hierarchy during the 1960s. Cynical, arrogant, and opportunistic, Novotný was the opposite of Dubček. Still, he was smart enough to realize that Dubček — competent, loyal to the party, and with few burning ambitions of his own — posed little threat to Novotný's position. So, when Dubček returned from Moscow, he was again promoted. In 1958, he became the regional party secretary for Bratislava.

Soviet tanks roll into Budapest in 1956. When Hungarians, eager for reform and hoping to rid their country of Soviet domination, staged an uprising in November of that year, Khrushchev sent in the tanks to quell the movement. Hundreds of reformers, including Hungarian reformer Imre Nagy, were killed.

A centuries-old city on the Danube River, Bratislava was Slovakia's traditional capital as well as the third-largest city in Czechoslovakia. His new appointment lifted Dubček out of the army of faceless gray bureaucrats from which party and government officials were culled. While still holding on to the Bratislava post, Dubček was also elected to the central committees of both the regional Slovak and the national Czechoslovak Communist parties. For a time, Novotný faced no challenges from Dubček, who still dutifully and conscientiously followed policies set down in Prague. One of the most controversial policies dealt with Slovak autonomy within the Czechoslovak state.

Slovaks still felt that they were not treated as equal partners with the Czechs. There had been some attempts, mostly unsuccessful, to address Slovak grievances. In the closing days of the war, a plan was drawn up in Kosice, Slovakia, between all the political leaders, including Communists, who were to form the postwar National Front. They agreed on the administrative and legislative structures to be established so that Slovak self-government could be assured. The Communist party itself had two wings: the all-embracing national Czechoslovak Communist party and the regional Slovak Communist party. Although the Slovak party operated fairly independently throughout the war, its activities were later folded into the Czechoslovak party. Still, it was intended that Slovak Communists would retain a substantial degree of autonomy.

Things turned out quite differently, however. As one of the principal targets of the purges in Czechoslovakia, Slovak Communists were accused of "bourgeois nationalism." They had defended their local and regional interests more than the central authorities liked. Curiously, the more dominant ethnic groups, such as the Russians in the Soviet Union or the Czechs in Czechoslovakia, were never so accused, even though most policies favored them at the expense of other groups.

The purges in the early 1950s thus removed most of the leading Slovak Communists who posed a challenge to Czechoslovak party leaders in Prague. They

> *Enjoyment? A politician does not know the meaning of the word. Moreover you never know what is going to happen next.*
> —NIKITA KHRUSHCHEV
> Soviet premier

were replaced by men who had little, if any, allegiance to Slovakia. By 1959, Novotný had reorganized the administration of the country so that the power of party officials on the most local levels was severely curbed. Regional party secretaries such as Dubček played a more expanded role than before, but given the overall administrative changes, the influence of the regions themselves was diminished, and in 1960, when Antonín Novotný revised the Czechoslovak constitution, Slovak autonomy was further chipped away. Several semiautonomous branches of the government in Slovakia were abolished; those that remained were turned into mere administrative bodies whose job it was to implement decisions made in Prague. Even the Slovak National Council was turned into little more than a rubber-stamp agency.

In his speeches, Dubček supported these moves and urged the angry Slovaks to fall in line behind the principle of "democratic centralism." He maintained that the "unity of the socialist camp is the guarantee of our progress. . . . We are indebted to the Czechoslovak Communist party for the creative way in which it has put the principles of Marxism-Leninism to work."

In 1960, Dubček made his first move from the regional to the national political arena. He was named to the secretariat of the Central Committee of the Czechoslovak Communist party in Prague, where he handled issues relating to industrial policy. In this position, Dubček witnessed the decline of Czechoslovakia's industry — a decline set in motion when a centralized Soviet-style economic system had been imposed after the Communist takeover of Czechoslovakia in 1948. In addition to the collectivization of agriculture and the nationalization of all previously private businesses, the economy was patterned after the Soviet Union's in a number of other ways. Heavy industry received enormous investment at the expense of the well-developed lighter industry that Czechoslovakia had built up before the war. Industrial production in Czechoslovakia sagged, partly because of unfair trade agreements and partly because economic de-

cisions were made by the Soviets with the interests of the Soviet Union, rather than those of Czechoslovakia, in mind.

This state of affairs was both poignant and bitter, especially in the Czech territories of Bohemia and Moravia. Before the war, they had enjoyed a successfully diversified economy with a high degree of industrialization. Then the label "Made in Czechoslovakia" had stood for high-quality products. Now those products were as shoddy as those manufactured by Czechoslovakia's less-developed neighbors.

Czechoslovakia's economy was in a state of crisis. Its gross national product — the measure of a country's total output of goods and services — had grown at a rate of 11 percent in 1959. Three years later, it was only 6.2 percent, and 1 year after that, in 1963, there was a further decline in the rate of growth.

Antonín Novotný became president of Czechoslovakia in 1957 after having served as first secretary of the Czechoslovak Communist party since 1953. Novotný was considered a brilliant administrator by his peers, but his blind adherence to party dogma evidenced a lack of imagination.

A Czechoslovak factory worker prepares a sack of sugar for export in 1957. Though Czechoslovakia had established itself as a leader in the sugar industry, during the late 1950s and 1960s the country's economy was in a state of crisis, and even its sugar production slowed.

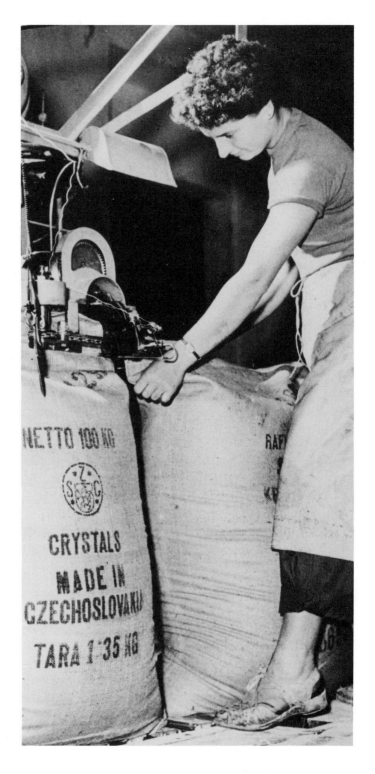

Again, Dubček first blamed human failings, rather than the centralized economic system, for the predicament. He believed that if only people would follow the Five-Year Plan — the economic blueprint by which the Communist governments of Eastern Europe directed their economies — then everything would work. In socialist economies following the Soviet model, the party, rather than market forces, decides what and how many goods are manufactured and which services are provided. But, because the party cannot anticipate all of the needs and demands of the economy, the system is inefficient. Even in his brief tenure as industry secretary, Dubček was faced daily with the reality that the Five-Year Plan was failing, and he began to view the Five-Year Plan with skepticism. Ironically, the push for economic reforms in Czechoslovakia came from the very source that was responsible for the country's economic crisis.

Because the Soviet Union was having economic difficulties of its own, Khrushchev allowed the ideas of an economist named Evsei Liberman to be heard. Liberman called for the reorganization of the Soviet economy. Liberman argued that factory managers, long under Moscow's thumb, should be given the power to make decisions without government intervention. Also, he urged the Soviet government to allow factories to make a profit and not limit production to quotas determined by the state.

Some of Liberman's ideas resonated in Czechoslovakia. A young economist named Ota Sik had been brought into the government in the early 1960s to formulate a blueprint for bringing the country out of its economic crisis. Sik's proposals were even more radical than Liberman's. He argued not only that decision making should be decentralized but also that market forces such as supply and demand should be allowed free play in the economy. Furthermore, he urged that price controls be lifted so that the true value of what was produced could be determined.

Novotný first allowed some of Sik's proposals to be publicized, and they quickly gained acceptance among other economists and some of the more re-

Lenin said that it is very
important to encourage all
citizens to take part in the
ruling of the State.
Representatives must
constantly meet their
constituents; they must really
understand thoroughly the
particular problems of the
districts they represent.
—ALEXANDER DUBČEK
in 1964

form-minded party leaders. However, his ideas met fierce resistance from rank-and-file apparatchiks, whose sole function was to implement decisions made by the central ministries. If the central ministries no longer were to make such decisions, there would be no need for the apparatchiks' jobs. Because of a huge outcry from this quarter, Novotný did not implement Sik's reforms. When he eventually agreed to some of them, his halfhearted measures assured that nothing changed. This frustrated Czechoslovakia's economists, who began to turn against Novotný.

Meanwhile, Khrushchev's call for de-Stalinization, so long ignored by Novotný, began to have a real impact on Czechoslovakia. In the early 1960s, Khrushchev mounted a new attack on Stalin, and this time it was much more difficult for Novotný to avoid doing the same. In contrast to Poland and Hungary, the truth about Stalinist excesses in Czechoslovakia had never been aired in public. Thousands of people had by now been released, but few had been rehabilitated. Thus, Czechoslovakia's need to reevaluate the past was building. People wanted to know the truth about the purges in their own country. They wanted Stalin's innocent victims rehabilitated and the Stalinists who had victimized them punished.

Spurred by the cultural thaw in the Soviet Union, Czechoslovakia's intellectuals were also emboldened to demand greater freedom of expression. During the early 1960s, novelists such as Milan Kundera and Ludvík Vaculik, playwrights such as Václav Havel, and filmmakers such as Milos Forman established international reputations for their work. Many of these works explored previously forbidden themes: For example, Slovak writer Ladislav Mnacko's *Taste of Power* lambasted the entrenched Communist bureaucracy.

With his tightly woven control of society now threatening to unravel, Novotný saw that he would have to make more than token gestures to appease these disparate forces. In order to save his own position, he had now to sacrifice the political careers of some of his trusted subordinates. In 1963, Novotný dismissed Karol Bacílek, who had been instrumental in conducting the purges 10 years earlier, and named Alexander Dubček, who had risen through the Slovak Communist party ranks, as first secretary of the Slovak Communist party — the most important job in Slovakia. Novotný would have preferred to place one of his own subordinates there, and at least once during Dubček's tenure Novotný tried to get him ousted. But Slovak Communists, tired of Novotný's arrogance and high-handedness, supported Dubček, and they did so even with certain reservations of their own. The poor economy, the clamor of the intellectuals for greater freedom of expression, the relative silence about the purges, and general Slovak discontent had converged to fuel the movement for reform; and, having sacrificed his own cronies, Novotný grew increasingly isolated within the country.

Then Novotný's predicament grew worse when he misread the political signals coming from Moscow. After resisting Khrushchev's reforms for so many years, Novotný began to initiate in Czechoslovakia policies that were about to be reversed in the Soviet Union. Khrushchev's reforms, although well intentioned, were poorly implemented and tended to alienate him from the powerful Soviet bureaucracy. When thousands of Soviet apparatchiks realized that the implementation of Khrushchev's reforms would do away with their privileged positions, they rebelled. Khrushchev was deposed by other members of the Soviet Communist party in October 1964, and Leonid Brezhnev became the party's new first secretary.

Novotný should have gotten along well with Brezhnev. Both men disliked Khrushchev's de-Stalinization efforts; both men were essentially apparatchiks who wanted to maintain their privileges and power but had little vision for how their countries should be run. However, Novotný had failed to appreciate Brezhnev's importance while Khrushchev was still in power and slighted him on more than one occasion. And when Khrushchev was deposed, Novotný spontaneously — and foolishly — called Brezhnev, demanding to know why he had not been

Soviet leaders (left to right) Nikita Khrushchev, Leonid Brezhnev, and Anastas Mikoyan attend a meeting of the Supreme Soviet in Moscow on December 6, 1961. In 1964, Brezhnev replaced Khrushchev as first secretary of the Communist party in the Soviet Union.

informed of these plans earlier. It was inappropriate behavior for a subordinate, and Brezhnev never forgot it. As Novotný's position became increasingly untenable in Czechoslovakia, he appealed to the Soviet leader for support, but Brezhnev had no desire to save him. When the move to oust Novotný grew serious in December 1967, Brezhnev went to Czechoslovakia. After speaking with Novotný and other Communist leaders, Brezhnev left abruptly, saying, "This is your affair." That sealed Novotný's fate.

Meanwhile, as the highest-ranked Communist official in the Slovak party between 1963 and 1967, Dubček underwent a major change in his thinking. He came to believe that reform was the only way to preserve the integrity of Communist ideals. No longer was the party sacrosanct in all respects. Dubček now believed that if the party made mistakes, then the party needed to own up to and take responsibility for them. Only in this way, he reasoned, would communism regain its credibility among the people, a credibility that had all but eroded in the two decades that the party had been in power.

Dubček was certainly not alone in his view. There were many Communists who had started out believing in the noble ideals of the party but had become seriously disillusioned. Many of these people were themselves victims of the purges. But they, too, were not ready to give up their belief in communism — they merely wanted to redefine it so that it would become more humane. One of the most persuasive voices for reform in Slovakia was Gustav Husák, who had been released from prison in 1960 and after a few years returned to Slovak Communist party affairs. Many of Husák's fellow purge victims formed the backbone of the reform movement that Dubček was to champion.

In 1967, Novotný, in a series of episodes in which he displayed a galling arrogance and an extraordinary lack of sensitivity, further managed to alienate those individuals already unhappy with him. Then, in late October, at a meeting of the party's Central Committee in Prague, Dubček blasted Novotný for his poor judgment and abuse of power. As more and more segments of society grew restive, calls for Novotný's ouster grew louder. The party itself split in factions, with the reformers, of whom Dubček was one, gaining strength against Novotný. By December, it was increasingly clear that Novotný had to go, and not even an official visit by Brezhnev was enough to save him. Novotný tried one last time to salvage his position: He tried to organize a military action against the reformers, hoping to arrest them by surprise and then try them on charges of counterrevolution. But Dubček found out about these plans and confronted Novotný with them, and the cornered leader was forced to call everything off.

Novotný was finally forced to step down on January 5, 1968. That day, Dubček was named first secretary of the Czechoslovak Communist party. With his mild, self-effacing demeanor, loyal track record, and reputation for fairness, Dubček was the choice that all the disparate factions in Czechoslovakia, sometimes united by little other than their distaste for Novotný, could accept. A few cynical party members also supported him because they believed that he could easily be manipulated. Given his rather unassuming past, no one expected him to introduce any radical changes. Certainly no one — least of all Dubček himself — expected him to champion a reform movement of great proportions.

6

Spring Is Here

When Dubček became first secretary of the Czechoslovak Communist party on January 5, 1968, most people still knew very little about him. Though more than 6 feet tall, the 46-year-old Dubček did not cut a dashing figure. He wore ill-fitting suits and was somewhat shy and nervous. His speeches were often long-winded and boring. Tad Szulc, the *New York Times* journalist then based in Prague, noted that "when he spoke publicly, Dubček was the epitome of unexcitement."

So there was not much on the surface to distinguish him from other Soviet bloc leaders who occasionally stepped into the shoes of a disgraced predecessor. The public images of these men were very much alike, while their private lives were scrupulously hidden from public view. They were glorified as humble, hardworking revolutionaries untouched by the corrupting wealth and privilege associated with capitalism. In the Communist world such glorification was dubbed the "cult of personality," whereby a leader was endowed with qualities of wisdom, foresight, goodness, honesty, and statesmanship.

I keep forgetting he is a Communist and I just think of him as a Czechoslovak man doing the right thing for our country.
—young woman at Prague University, commenting about Dubček in the spring of 1968

A jubilant Alexander Dubček embodies the spirit of Prague Spring in May 1968. After 20 years of oppressive Soviet domination of Czechoslovakia, Dubček, calling for "socialism with a human face," replaced Novotný as first secretary of the Czechoslovak Communist party and brought hope to a country plagued with political and economic problems.

In reality, none of these leaders lived up to his public image. Most lived lives far removed from the ordinary workers they supposedly championed. Leonid Brezhnev, for example, owned half a dozen luxury foreign cars and had at his disposal several spacious residences, whereas the majority of Soviet families were crammed into tiny 2-room apartments and waited up to 15 years to buy a poorly made Soviet automobile. Antonín Novotný shared Brezhnev's taste. He regularly—and illegally—dipped into Czechoslovakia's state reserves of Western currency to buy luxury items.

Alexander Dubček eschewed such practices. Even when he was the highest-ranking Communist in Slovakia, he walked to work every morning from his Bratislava home, forgoing the chauffeured limousine that was a matter of course for Novotný in Prague. Moreover, Anna Dubček, unlike the wives of other high party officials, had no live-in maid. She did her own shopping and was helped with housework by a charlady who came by only occasionally. When Dubček got Novotný's job, the family stayed in their modest five-room house in Bratislava. Dubček took a room in the party hotel in Prague, commuting home on the weekends. Like his colleagues, Dubček hoped to keep reports about his personal life from becoming public, believing such information to be inappropriate and unimportant. But unlike them, he had nothing to hide. His public image was a true reflection of his private life.

Such details already hinted at what made Dubček different. He abhorred the cult of personality. For him, communism was not a means to inflate his own sense of importance or to gain material advantages. He was a true believer surrounded by cynical apparatchiks who had long forgotten, if they ever knew, what the spirit of communism was supposed to be about. Dubček wanted to return the party to the idealism it had managed to trample and dismiss during its 20 years in power.

During his first days in office, however, he had no idea how he would do this. He had no firm mandate, having become leader simply because no one

In his new position of power, Dubček spent weeks reading state documents and reports and consulting with his advisers. Eventually he devised a program that he hoped would restore social and economic freedom to a country long shackled by the Soviet Communists.

else was as acceptable to all the factions opposed to Novotný. Dubček now sought to inform himself as much as possible about the real state of affairs in Czechoslovakia. For the first three weeks of January 1968, he read scores of reports and consulted with dozens of advisers and experts. He called on many of the country's leading intellectuals. Here he already showed a difference in style from Novotný. Both Dubček and Novotný were pragmatic men, skilled in political maneuvering yet not particularly inclined toward intellectual pursuits. But Novotný despised intellectuals, whereas Dubček respected them — even those who were not members of the Communist party — and solicited their opinions. They, in turn, provided Dubček with the theoretical underpinnings and factual analysis he needed to fashion a truly audacious reform program.

What made the Czechoslovak experience a true 20th-century revolution was that it undertook to wed socialist concepts of social economic justice with the West's traditions of political, cultural, and scientific freedom.

—TAD SZULC
journalist

Dubček also had help from his reform-minded colleagues within the party and the government. They included Presidium members Josef Spacek and Oldrich Cernik. (In early April, Cernik was appointed prime minister, and five men, including economist Ota Sik and Slovak reformer Gustav Husák, were appointed deputy prime ministers.) Central Committee member and onetime purge victim Josef Smrkovsky and Dubček's close associate and political-ideology aide Zdenek Mlynar were even more closely identified with the reforms than Dubček was himself. There were many others in less prominent positions who helped Dubček.

However, not everyone was supportive. A full one-third of the 100-member Central Committee had voted against Dubček's succeeding Novotný, and almost all of those party members and government officials who opposed the reforms remained in their old positions. Even Novotný, forced to step down as Communist party leader, still retained the largely ceremonial but nevertheless prestigious post of president. Dubček did not institute a wide-scale sweep of officials, something that usually happened with a change in leadership, and this soon worked to his detriment. Novotný used what remained of his influence to try to undermine Dubček's new policies. Later during the winter of 1968, however, Novotný's role in the attempted coup against the reformers the previous December was uncovered. In May, he was thrown out of the party. Ludvík Svoboda, a purge victim who had fought alongside the Soviet Red Army during World War II, was named president.

In late January, Dubček made a courtesy visit to Moscow, which was customary for new Eastern European Communist leaders. There he met with Leonid Brezhnev and other members of the Soviet Politburo. The official Soviet communiqué stated that the talks underscored "warm friendship, sincerity, and complete identity of views on all matters discussed." Then Dubček met with his counterparts in two neighboring Communist countries, Władysław Gomułka of Poland and János Kádár of Hungary. Along with East Germany's Walter Ulbricht and Bulgaria's Todor Zhivkov, these men—alarmed that the Czech reform experiment could be exported to their own countries—would in only a few months call for Dubček's head. But in late January, everything was smiles and solidarity.

By early February, Dubček sounded the first public intimations of what was to come. In a speech at the Seventh Congress of Unified Agricultural Cooperatives, Dubček called on the country's farmers to help shape their own future. It was a radical departure from the traditional party line, which had claimed for itself all decision-making rights in practically every sphere of life. "Democracy is not only the right and chance to pronounce one's own views, but also the way in which people's views are handled," he told the 1,800 delegates at the congress. "Government organs must strive to create the optimum conditions in which farmers can apply their skills and initiative, not to give orders on when and how to reap and sow."

Under the watchful eye of Lenin and Gottwald, Dubček applauds with (left to right) Soviet leader Brezhnev, Czechoslovak Communist party leaders Jaromir Dolansky and Antonín Novotný, and East German leader Walter Ulbricht at a party meeting in Prague Castle on February 22, 1968.

Dubček tips his hat to a massive crowd of admirers in April 1968. Dubček earned the support of the masses not only with his reforms but with his charm and warmth. Having known only the stern Communist bureaucrats of recent decades, the Czechoslovak people recognized Dubček as a man of humble compassion.

The wary farmers did not quite know what to make of their new leader. While not eloquent, he spoke sincerely, transmitting a warmth never seen in the bombastic Novotný. What Dubček said was likewise startling. For years, the farmers' freedom had been taken away from them by the Communist party — first by collectivization, then by economic control exercised by the central ministries. Now here was this very same party's highest representative saying they had a right to their own voices. Cautiously, they began to use them. One after another, farmers stood up to ask hard questions and

to complain about their difficulties. Dubček told them about his plans for an "Action Program," which would be the official document outlining the reforms he envisioned.

Open forums such as this took place all over the country, in village and town halls, at the schools and universities, in the factories and offices. People began to say what they truly thought. Students, workers, professionals, intellectuals, and party members discussed their frustrations and concerns openly for the first time in 20 years. It was both exhilarating and frightening.

Young street poets and musicians entertain a crowd of onlookers during Prague Spring. In the late 1960s, the voice of social and political reformers was heard throughout Western Europe and the United States as well as in Czechoslovakia.

The long silence imposed upon Czechoslovakia had produced bitter feelings. Yet during Czechoslovakia's national awakening, which took place from January to August 1968, a period that came to be known as Prague Spring, few people called for revenge. A public opinion poll published in early May, for example, showed that while 90 percent of the population supported fully rehabilitating the victims of the purges, only 58 percent wanted to bring their past oppressors to trial. Czechoslovaks simply yearned for a more just way of doing things in their country so that they could live with dignity and without fear.

Intellectuals, particularly writers, shaped much of the public discussion. By the end of February, censorship had stopped on its own in Czechoslovakia. The censorship apparatus, found in every publishing house, newspaper, or magazine, needed to have a direct and constant tie to the party leadership in order to understand, at any one given point in time, what was and was not permissible to say or write. After Dubček became leader in January, such directives simply no longer appeared. Censors still existed, but they had nothing to do. Having no guidance, they often ended up playing cards with each other or fetching coffee for the journalists and editors whose work they had so recently had the power to veto.

Czechoslovakia's journalists quickly stepped into the vacuum. Up until then, they had been largely a group of undistinguished conformists. Now emboldened, they wrote and broadcast reports that addressed the most controversial issues of the day. The public caught on quickly. By March, newspapers were sold out at the kiosks by 7:30 in the morning. The trade union daily, *Prace*, doubled its circulation in Prague, but that still fell short of demand. The combined circulation of Prague's seven major dailies more than quadrupled between January and March. The Union of Czech Writers wrested back from the Ministry of Culture the weekly publication *Literary Noviny* (Literary News), which Novotný had placed under government control. It became *Literary Listy* (Literary Letters), the first issue of which was published in February. Already popular during Novotný's days, with a circulation of 56,000, *Literary Listy* would sell 300,000 copies per week in 1968.

In late January, the Union of Czech Writers met in Prague. The tone of this meeting was radically different from one held a mere half year earlier, when Novotný attempted to squash the more rebellious members. A new breed of official, such as novelist Milan Kundera — long relegated to the shadows — was elected by the writers. The new chairman was Eduard Goldstuecker. Originally arrested and tried with Rudolf Slánský during the purges in the early 1950s, Goldstuecker was one of three men who escaped execution and was sentenced to life imprisonment instead. Quietly released some years earlier, Goldstuecker was crucial in the early 1960s in rehabilitating Czechoslovakia's greatest modern novelist, Franz Kafka, who had died in 1924. Now Goldstuecker himself was not only rehabilitated but also elected by his fellow writers to a very prominent position.

Soon other heroes, long consigned to oblivion by the Communist party bosses, were rehabilitated. Pictures of Tomáš Masaryk and Edvard Beneš suddenly appeared in bookshop windows. Older people who had remembered them from the days of Czechoslovakia's democracy wept with joy.

Though Dubček did not always initiate these changes, none of them could have come about without his blessing. Dubček believed that the party's responsibility was to allow all people, non-Communists included, to have a voice in how the country was to be run. He would even call for non-Communists to be allowed to participate in government, effectively ending the Communist party's monopoly on power. It was this that most frightened and infuriated Leonid Brezhnev and Czechoslovakia's neighboring Communist leaders. For them, to share power with others meant to give it up completely. The way they saw it, Dubček was actively helping to eradicate the Communist party's institutionalized, codified right to a leading role in the country. No amount of counterargument from Dubček — who had no intention of allowing the Communist party in Czechoslovakia to be pushed aside —did anything to convince them otherwise.

Dubček's agenda for reform did not always match that of the more ardent Czechoslovak reformers. Making the Communist party popular and credible was not a goal that everyone shared. Many did not feel much loyalty to a party that had been the cause of such personal as well as national misfortune. Throughout Prague Spring, there would be an underlying tension between the radicals who pushed for greater reform at a faster pace and Dubček, who tried to steer a more central course. On several oc-

You thought that here, in our Republic, the Soviet Union was in the driver's seat. If anyone is still thinking that, my young friends, he is terribly wrong. Those times are behind us, Comrades, our relations are now built on the principle of equality, on the principle of sovereignty.
—JOSEF SMRKOVSKY addressing students after a hockey match at the Olympic Games in February 1968, when the Czechs beat the Soviets

casions, he publicly stated that he would not tolerate either reactionaries or "the enemies of socialism" taking advantage of his reforms. Thus, in March, many activists were still tentative, telling foreign reporters that "for the time being, we are behind Dubček."

But both Dubček and the more radical reformers were united in the conviction that the truth needed to be told about the reality of Czechoslovak life, and they agreed that the appropriate place to begin was with a reassessment of the purges of the 1950s.

A forceful Dubček speaks emphatically at a Communist party meeting in March 1968. Though Dubček's democratic reforms had enormous popular support, his policies got mixed reviews from his Communist party colleagues, many of whom were hard-liners eager to please the Soviets.

The party relies on the voluntary support of the people. The party cannot impose its authority by force but must constantly earn it by its deeds. The party cannot carry out its line by command but only through the work of its members and through the truthfulness of its ideals.

—ALEXANDER DUBČEK
from his Action Program

Friends recalled that in January, when Dubček first gained access to the confidential archives, he was horrified by what he learned.

Some years before, Novotný had appointed a commission to explore the illegalities alleged to have occurred during the purges, but it had been just a token gesture, and nothing had been done about the findings. Now many purge victims spoke of their ordeal publicly for the first time, and scores of articles appeared in the press. In April, a commission headed by Presidium member Jan Piller was set up to fully document the purges. Some former purge victims themselves formed a self-help group, called the K 231, named after the statute under which they had been unjustly charged and sentenced. The group served as a center for collecting information about political prisoners.

Throughout the spring, the government drafted preliminary laws. These sought not only to rehabilitate the victims of the purges by restoring their good names but also, when possible, to provide some material compensation for them and their families. It was estimated that over 100,000 cases needed to be reexamined. In June, the principal rehabilitation law was passed, and the actual process was projected to begin the following September. But this plan, the first of its kind to be implemented by a Communist government, was never carried out.

On April 10, Dubček published a 51-page document summarizing the Action Program and making his plan official party policy. Work on the Action Program had begun in early February, when Dubček urged that the party rank and file and regional organizations contribute to its formulation. Dubček wanted to make the Action Program a truly representative document from the Czechoslovak party. In previous years, it was the party's dozen or so Presidium members who set policy. The lower echelons were simply supposed to carry it out obediently. As radical as Dubček's break from past practice was, however, it still was far from being truly democratic. Non-Communists had no part in putting together the Action Program, even though it was a blueprint for changing the political, economic, and social course of the entire country.

Still, the Action Program was where Dubček officially set down his view that non-Communist parties should be allowed to participate in political life. He did not envision them as opposition parties but rather as helpers to the Communist party, which would of course retain its leading role. The vehicle he hoped to use was the National Front, the coalition of six political parties first established at the end of World War II. After the Communist takeover in 1948, the National Front had ceased to have any relevance. But its structural shell still existed, and Dubček wanted to revive it.

Far more startlingly, however, the Action Program called for the right of all citizens to free expression and free assembly, and it promised to guarantee these rights by amendments to the constitution. Censorship was to be curtailed. The right to travel, even to live abroad, and the right to seek restitution from the illegal seizure of one's property were also addressed. The structure of government between the Czech lands and Slovakia was to be altered so that Slovak self-government was a reality, not just a paper nicety. The economy would also be restructured to guarantee the emergence of a market (a socialist market, to be sure, not a capitalist one), and business enterprises were to be granted far more independence than before. Also, trade with Western capitalist countries was to be expanded.

That Dubček saw his reforms as socialist developments and not capitalist ones was underscored by his reiteration of Czechoslovakia's continued close military and political alliance with the Soviet Union. Unlike Hungary's Imre Nagy in 1956, Dubček had no intention of pulling Czechoslovakia out of the Warsaw Pact. Neither did he wish to make the Czechoslovak experiment a model for the other Warsaw Pact countries to follow. He insisted that it was tailored to specific Czechoslovak conditions and thought it arrogant to suggest that it might be applicable elsewhere. Although Dubček might not have intended it, this was an indirect criticism of the Soviet Union: Soviet leaders operated on the assumption that the Soviet model of socialism was the only model for Eastern Europe. Dubček had clearly stepped over the line.

7

Tanks Bring Winter

May Day, the holiday honoring the workers of the world, was enthusiastically celebrated for the first time in Czechoslovakia in 1968. More than 100,000 people filled the streets that May 1. Before, May Day had been an obligatory event in which people participated because they were forced to. But in 1968 in Czechoslovakia, their enthusiasm was genuine.

Dubček was everyone's man of the hour. Unknown even by his own people just a few short months before, he was by now an international figure. Even the Communist parties of the Western countries — particularly Italy — were enthusiastic about political developments in Czechoslovakia. In Eastern Europe, Yugoslavia's Tito and Romania's new leader, Nicolae Ceauşescu, were alone in supporting Dubček. (Ironically, Romania's Ceauşescu was later to become a dictator so brutal in his own country that he would be more hated than Stalin.)

After the Russian invasion of 1968, every Czech was confronted with the thought that his nation could be quietly erased from Europe.
—MILAN KUNDERA
Czech writer

Though he enjoyed celebrity status during the summer of 1968, Dubček began to be concerned about the future of his reform program. Dubček knew that the Soviets would not sit idly by and watch the democratization of socialism take place in Czechoslovakia.

Dubček and Czechoslovak president Ludvík Svoboda lead a May Day parade through the streets of Prague in 1968. Whereas in the past Czechoslovaks had to be "persuaded" by the Communist party to attend the festivities held each year on May 1 to honor workers, during Prague Spring the people turned out in droves.

Stories about the Czech experiment dominated the newspapers and magazines of the Western press week after week, and Dubček's picture appeared on the cover of *Time* magazine. Reporters followed his every move and witnessed the enormous popularity Dubček enjoyed. Whereas most Communist leaders hid behind formal facades and official slogans, Dubček mingled with the crowds. He was photographed cheering for his favorite soccer team in Bratislava

and signing his autograph for dozens of waiting children. He talked to people on the street easily and frankly, answering whatever questions they put to him and taking notes on the comments and problems that they had. His accessibility and lack of pretension won them over. For example, when he announced that gold reserves in Czechoslovakia were low, thousands of women donated their gold wedding bands to the government.

Dubček's family was extraordinarily proud of him. Anna Dubček, however, was also concerned. She cared little for the prestige of being the wife of the country's leader and worried that the pressures Dubček was under would prove too much of a strain. From the time he took office in January, Dubček worked 16- to 18-hour days and often slept only 4 hours a night. Because of this rigorous schedule, he lost 28 pounds in 8 months.

Leonid Brezhnev did not share in Czechoslovakia's euphoria. As early as February, when he came to Prague to commemorate the 20th anniversary of Communist rule in the country, Brezhnev had made his displeasure known. The Soviet ambassador and informants in the Czechoslovak government had kept him apprised of events, which to him smacked not so much of reform as they did of counterrevolution. Dubček dealt with Brezhnev by trying to appease him. As he told a friend, "I just try to smile at Brezhnev as he shouts at me. I say yes, yes, I agree and then I come home and do nothing."

This approach began to wear on Brezhnev's patience. Dubček was called to face Brezhnev and the other four Soviet bloc leaders several times between March and August 1968. In late March, he went to Dresden, East Germany, to answer charges that the Czechoslovak press was fomenting dangerous anti-Communist sentiment. Dubček agreed that restraint had to be exercised, for he, too, was concerned that the reforms he introduced could be exploited by those intent on defeating communism. Upon returning to Prague, though, Dubček did not censor the press but simply implored journalists not to antagonize the Soviet Union.

This soft approach did not work. While the writers and journalists understood Dubček's predicament, they believed that self-censorship of this kind ran counter to the idea of a free press, which to them meant that all views could now be aired, including those that were critical of the Communist party and of the Soviet Union. Moreover, if Dubček clamped down on the press, he would be obstructing the very reforms he was trying to introduce. In late May, writer Ludvík Vaculik published a manifesto called

> *Human socialism, then, was the philosophy of the Czechoslovak revolution, and it was a tragedy for Marxism and socialism that Brezhnev's tanks temporarily interrupted this East European renaissance before it could be fully and freely tested.*
> —TAD SZULC
> journalist

The 2,000 Words, in which he wrote that the Communist party "which after the war possessed the great trust of the people, gradually exchanged this trust for offices, until it had all offices and nothing else. . . . The incorrect line of the leadership changed the party from a political party and an ideological alliance into a power organization that became very attractive to egotists avid for rule, calculating cowards, and unprincipled people." *The 2,000 Words* was the most stinging broadside yet published against the party. That 70 of Czechoslovakia's leading intellectuals and thousands of its citizens signed it added to its power.

Brezhnev read *The 2,000 Words* in Moscow just hours after it was published in Czechoslovakia. He immediately telephoned Dubček and directed him to condemn the manifesto publicly.

Dubček was now clearly in serious trouble. Attacks on his reform policies in Czechoslovakia began to appear in the Soviet press and increased in number and intensity throughout the spring. More ominously, the Soviets announced in May that they planned to conduct "routine" military maneuvers on Czechoslovak and Polish soil to test Warsaw Pact "combat readiness." Dubček could not refuse. Later, the bewildered Czechoslovak Defense Ministry reported that the Soviet units were actually "bringing in special signal equipment which we ourselves will use for our own maneuvers later in the year." Indeed, special signal equipment was brought in — but it was the Soviets themselves who would use it before the summer was out.

Throughout June, the nervous Czechoslovaks continued their reforms while Soviet tanks rumbled through Czechoslovakia's countryside. At first there were supposed to be only about 3,000 Soviet soldiers involved, but by the time the maneuvers ended in early July, an estimated 16,000 Soviet soldiers had taken part.

In mid-July, Brezhnev and the other four Communist leaders sent Dubček a letter demanding that he come to Warsaw, answer questions about *The 2,000 Words*, and halt the reforms at home immediately. Dubček politely refused. Brezhnev then

> *The bloody massacre in Bangladesh quickly covered the memory of the Russian invasion of Czechoslovakia, the assassination of Allende drowned out the groans of Bangladesh, the war in the Sinai Desert made people forget Allende, the Cambodian massacre made people forget Sinai, and so on and so forth until ultimately everyone lets everything be forgotten.*
> —MILAN KUNDERA
> Czech writer

Dubček (right) and Soviet leader Brezhnev join hands, smile, and gesture to a cheering crowd in Bratislava in August 1968, giving the impression that all is well between their two countries. However, darker political forces were at work.

wrote a stinging missive signed by the other four leaders as well — it came to be known as the Warsaw Letter — wherein he charged that the Czechoslovak reforms were a betrayal of socialism and the Communist party and that the Soviet Union was prepared to act.

In late July, Dubček met with Brezhnev in Cierna nad Tisou, a Czechoslovak border town. For four days, Brezhnev raged at Dubček for hours at a time and tried to turn the Czech leaders against one another. Dubček had publicly promised the Czechoslovak people that he would not give in to Soviet pressure, and so he did not concede anything. The result was a stalemate: The two sides agreed that they would sign a rather meaningless document in Bratislava a few days later, reaffirming their common purpose in furthering the socialist cause. As he returned to Prague, Dubček believed he had averted disaster one more time.

But Dubček's luck had finally run out. At 10:30 P.M. on August 20, as controllers at Prague's Ruzyne Airport settled in for a quiet night, a Soviet warplane landed, and uniformed men climbed out. They were met by a waiting automobile. Soon, another Soviet plane appeared on the horizon, followed by another, and another. The sky filled with planes. On cue, men waiting in the airport lounge drew revolvers and burst into the control room. They ordered the startled controllers to give up their posts. The invasion of Czechoslovakia had begun.

Before the night was over, more than 200,000 troops from the five Warsaw Pact countries — the Soviet Union, Bulgaria, East Germany, Poland, and Hungary — crossed the Czechoslovak border at 18 different points. (They would be joined by an additional 300,000 troops the following week. At its peak, there would be some 650,000 Warsaw Pact soldiers in Czechoslovakia in late August. Czechoslovakia had a military force of only 175,000 men.) In the early morning hours of August 21, as the Czechoslovaks rubbed the sleep from their eyes, the rumble of tanks awakened them to the fact that the worst had happened. By dawn, the Soviets occupied Prague.

On the night of August 20, 1968, Soviet and other Warsaw Pact tanks rolled into Prague and put an abrupt end to the great hope that had been Prague Spring. By morning, Czechoslovakia was once again an occupied country.

Peter Dubček, the Czechoslovak leader's 19-year-old son, was vacationing in Egypt when the Soviets invaded his country in August 1968. On the advice of his mother, he remained in Egypt until September of that year.

For months, people had speculated that the Russians would use violence to halt the reforms, but still they were stunned when it finally happened — everyone, that is, except about 50 people in Prague who had known about the planned invasion well in advance. Though, of course, Dubček had no warning, the highest-ranking hard-line Czech and Slovak Communist party members who were against Dubček's reforms had not only been aware of the Soviet plan to invade Czechoslovakia but had participated in implementing it. Excluded from the forefront of political events in Czechoslovakia by the reformers, these bureaucrats secretly helped the Soviets, hoping to regain power.

Dubček was meeting with other Presidium members in the Central Committee building on the night of August 20 when he learned about the invasion. They were discussing the upcoming 14th Party Congress and the dilemma of how to stop anti-Communist propaganda in the press. When Prime Minister Cernik broke the news, Dubček blanched and said, "I declare on my honor as a Communist I had no suspicion, no indication, that anyone wanted to undertake such measures against us." An emergency proclamation was then drafted, but by the time Prague Radio was ready to broadcast it, the Czech hard-liners in conspiracy with the Soviets were able to stop it. In the early morning hours, several Soviet military vehicles pulled up to the Central Committee building. Dubček, Smrkovsky, and a handful of other officials were arrested and flown to the Soviet Union, where they were imprisoned.

In the immediate aftermath of the invasion, no one knew where Dubček was or if he was dead or alive. Dubček's family was frantic with worry. Anna and two of the Dubčeks' sons, on vacation in Yugoslavia when the invasion occurred, hurried back. (A third son, Peter, was in Egypt. He was advised to stay there and returned home only in early September.) Pavlina Dubček ran from one stone-faced official to another, pleading, "What have you done to my son?" But she got no answer.

In military terms, the invasion of Czechoslovakia was an unqualified success for Leonid Brezhnev.

The tanks and troops quickly occupied key posts — the Czechoslovak military bases, transportation crossings, and communications facilities. But in political terms, the invasion was a dismal failure. Brezhnev had hoped to create the illusion that the Czechoslovak people had welcomed the Warsaw Pact troops as liberators from the "counterrevolution." They did not. Although they heeded the Czechoslovak leadership's call not to fight, the people did everything else in their power to show how unwelcome the invaders were. Spontaneous demonstrations occurred; crowds hurled insults at the troops. They tore down street signs, replacing them with signs reading Dubček Boulevard or Svoboda Square so that the foreign soldiers, relying on maps, would lose their way around the cities, towns, and villages.

A young protester displays a torn, bloodstained Czechoslovakian flag as Warsaw Pact troops nonchalantly roll through the streets of Prague. Dubček was not allowed to remain in Czechoslovakia during the invasion; he was arrested and whisked to Moscow, where he was temporarily detained in a prison cell.

A young Czechoslovak woman shouts at Soviet occupying troops in Prague in August 1968. Brezhnev had hoped to create the impression that the Soviet forces were liberators, but the Czechoslovak people were not so gullible.

Young men climbed on tanks and stuck sticky paper on the visors, temporarily immobilizing them. With only three days' supply of food, the provisions for the invaders soon ran out, but the Czechoslovaks refused even to give them water. Though the invading forces were under strict orders to show restraint, in the first week alone, at least 186 people were killed, and more than 360 were seriously wounded.

The country's journalists held the nation together. Whenever one radio station was occupied, facilities were moved to another makeshift, secret location. Uncensored broadcasts continued behind the back of the occupying forces — in apartments, cinemas, or factories — keeping the people informed and morale high. The 14th Congress, scheduled for September, was hastily called together and held in a secret location in Prague, with hundreds of delegates attending — and the Soviets were unable to detect it. The congress resolved unequivocally to stand behind Dubček and the other arrested leaders.

On August 23, President Svoboda and a number of remaining officials flew to Moscow to negotiate the release of Dubček and the others. He also brought Dubček the news that the people of Czechoslovakia were united in their resistance against the invasion. Brezhnev had intended to impose a new leadership of conservative hard-liners on the country, but in the face of such fierce unity on the side of the people and Dubček's reformist colleagues, this plan fell apart. The conservatives were not yet strong enough to take over. Brezhnev accepted the fact that he had to allow Dubček to remain Czechoslovakia's leader, at least for the time being.

Brezhnev also had to endure the enormous criticism that rained down on him from around the world: The Western democracies all condemned the Soviet invasion of Czechoslovakia. But Brezhnev had guessed correctly that they would do little more than that. More disturbing to him was the reaction of the Communist parties around the world. Many,

Passersby notice the exclamation "Viva Dubček" written on a Prague wall. In the aftermath of the Soviet invasion of Czechoslovakia, such openly defiant political statements were punishable by imprisonment.

The people clamor for news. In late August 1968, with the radio and press heavily censored by the Soviets, Czechoslovak printers and journalists resorted to distributing newsletters on the streets of Prague.

especially in Western Europe, lashed out against the invasion. Brezhnev was in the midst of planning an international conference of all the Communist parties — those in power, those in opposition, and those underground. Worried by the Chinese Communists, who posed a threat to the Soviet Union in the Communist world movement, Brezhnev had hoped to use the conference to reassert Soviet preeminence. The invasion of Czechoslovakia did little to help this effort. When the conference was finally held in Moscow in June 1969, it was a dismal failure. Only 75 out of 111 Communist parties attended. Of the 14 ruling parties, 5 (Yugoslavia, Albania, China, North Korea, and North Vietnam) boycotted the conference. Others that did attend forced the Soviets to make certain concessions, highlighting criticism of Soviet policies. Instead of successfully reestablishing unquestioned Soviet dominance, the conference merely underscored the growing resistance to it.

Brezhnev nevertheless justified the invasion of Czechoslovakia by maintaining that communism had been in danger of collapsing there. In September 1968, *Pravda* published what came to be called the "Brezhnev Doctrine" by Western commentators. The article stated, "Every Communist party is responsible not only to its own people, but also to all socialist countries. . . . Communists in fraternal countries could not allow themselves to remain inactive while watching one of their number fall into the process of antisocialist degeneration."

Brezhnev had succeeded in stamping out "antisocialist degeneration" in Czechoslovakia: When Dubček returned on August 26, five days after the invasion, Prague Spring was dead. In Moscow, under pressure from the Soviets, Dubček had agreed to enforce tighter controls within Czechoslovakia and to cut back on trade with the West. Back home, in an emotional television broadcast to the nation, Dubček pleaded with the people for restraint and understanding. At several points in his speech, he paused, his voice choked by tears. He hoped to preserve as much of the reforms as possible, he told them. But in all truth, Dubček could no longer promise anything.

> *I did not think he could rise so high—a man like this, as good as this.*
> —LADSILAV MNACKO
> self-exiled Slovak writer,
> on Dubček

In April 1969, Gustav Husák replaced Dubček as first secretary of the Czechoslovak Communist party. Once a radical reformer, Husák now presided over the dismantling of the democratization program he and Dubček had bravely instituted together less than a year before.

Czechoslovakia's principal reformers soon went the way of Prague Spring; many suffered political attack before resigning their posts and disappearing from public life. At first, Dubček was not singled out for attack, but it was only a matter of time before he would be. While the hard-liners reasserted themselves and several reformers softened their positions, Dubček lost his power base.

The hopes of the Czechoslovaks turned to despair, exemplified on January 16, 1969, when a 21-year-old student named Jan Palach doused himself with gasoline, lit a match, and burned himself to death in an act of protest. He became an instant martyr, a symbol of Czechoslovakia's sorrow. To those who sought to "normalize" the society in the aftermath of the invasion, such martyrdom was unacceptable. The authorities, hoping to prevent Palach's grave from becoming a shrine, moved his body to another burial site.

On April 17, 1969, Dubček was replaced by Gustav Husák as first secretary of the Czechoslovak

Communist party. Husák had made numerous concessions to the Soviets and was now clearly a collaborator. Later that month, Dubček was named chairman of the Federal Assembly, and he was in that post on August 20, 1969, the first anniversary of the Soviet invasion. To commemorate the event, crowds gathered spontaneously in Prague's Wenceslas Square, shouting "At Zije Dubček!" (Long Live Dubček!). The police moved in to put down the demonstration. Half a dozen people were killed, and some 1,400 were arrested. This was the pretext used by the government to impose emergency laws suspending civil liberties. As chairman of the Federal Assembly, Dubček had to sign the laws into effect —a bitter twist.

Dubček was relieved of his Federal Assembly position in October 1969, and in January 1970 he was appointed ambassador to Turkey. It was rumored that the leadership hoped Dubček would use the opportunity to defect to the West, but he did not. Instead, for the six months he was ambassador, Dubček was a virtual prisoner in his own embassy. When he met with other diplomats, he was frequently under the watchful eye of the Soviet ambassador. The same was true for Anna Dubček. With their three sons still in Czechoslovakia, the couple's every move was monitored and controlled. On May 25, 1970, Dubček was thrown out of the Communist party and recalled to Prague. By now, the public attacks on him were unrelenting and vicious. On Prague Radio, Dubček was called "a renegade, traitor, revisionist, and failure."

Stefan Dubček died in May 1969. He had lived long enough to see his son fall from power but never wavered in supporting him. "I am very proud of him," he told foreign journalists a few months before his death, adding that "were Lenin alive today, he would approve of what my son has done."

The retribution against the reformers began in earnest in the early 1970s. Tens of thousands of liberals fled the country in the first months after the invasion; 500,000 of the 1 million Communist party members — almost a full one-third — were expelled by the end of 1970; some 7,000 officers were

Following the Soviet invasion of Czechoslovakia, Dubček vanished from his country's political arena. He took a job as a mechanic for the state Forestry Department in Bratislava, where he worked until 1981.

dismissed from the armed forces; and 40 percent of the country's journalists had lost their jobs by the end of 1972. Academics, actors, writers, government officials, and others who had supported Dubček's reforms lost their jobs or emigrated. In the 1970s, Czechoslovakia was a country where former professors were window washers, former ministers were janitors, and prominent writers took jobs as hospital orderlies.

Dubček retreated to Bratislava and became a mechanic for the Forestry Department. After being expelled from the Communist party, he was never mentioned in official media except to be vilified. His picture was airbrushed out of the official photographs. Although technically free, Dubček was constantly watched and followed by the security police. Former associates were discreetly warned not to visit him, and he socialized with only his family and his closest friends.

Dubček refused to be interviewed by the few intrepid foreign journalists who sought him out. Though subjected to constant harassment by the secret police and urged by the party leadership to "admit" that Prague Spring was a mistake, Dubček maintained that he had always acted with his country's best interest in mind and that Prague Spring was a glorious moment in Czechoslovakia's history. Although thrown out of the party, he still believed himself to be a loyal Communist.

Dubček vanished from the world stage, and by the time the 10th anniversary of the invasion rolled around in August 1978, Dubček had been a mechanic far longer than he had been a world leader. Young Czechoslovaks hardly knew anything about him. They were too young to remember Prague Spring — the time when, in Dubček's words, "we began to trust the people and they began to trust us." And the history books did not tell the story.

8

With a Human Face

In 1981, at age 60, Dubček retired from his job as a mechanic with the Forestry Department in Bratislava. The following year, his old nemesis Leonid Brezhnev died. After Brezhnev's immediate successors — Yuri Andropov and Konstantin Chernenko — also died in quick succession, a man from a younger generation, Mikhail Gorbachev, took over in 1985 as leader of the Soviet Union. The Soviet Union was in deep trouble economically, and Gorbachev needed to make it productive again. For that to happen, he concluded that the Soviet system had to become more democratic. So, soon after he took office, Gorbachev announced a two-pronged approach for solving his country's problems. People needed to be able to voice their opinions, Gorbachev reasoned, if they were to overhaul the system in order to make it more efficient. He popularized the Russian terms of *glasnost* (openness) and *perestroika* (restructuring) to describe the reforms he envisioned. As always, the policies of the Soviet leader

> *Where Socialism is concerned, in the end, the people must reign; they cannot be the object of a reign.*
> —ALEXANDER DUBČEK

Though he was forced out of public life in June 1970, when he was expelled from the Communist party, Dubček remained a symbol of hope and freedom for the people of Czechoslovakia. His effort to give socialism a human face was never forgotten.

Soviet leader Mikhail Gorbachev and his wife, Raisa, are greeted by workers during a visit to a West German steel mill in 1989. Many politicos consider Gorbachev's *perestroika* and *glasnost* — concepts on which the Soviet leader has built a monumental reform movement in his country — to be derived from ideas central to Dubček's Action Program of the 1960s.

would eventually have profound repercussions beyond that country's borders. So it had been with Stalin, Khrushchev, and Brezhnev; so it would be with Gorbachev.

To Dubček, glasnost and perestroika sounded very much like "socialism with a human face." In an interview with the Italian Communist newspaper *L'Unita* in January 1988, he said, "With all my heart, mind, and conscience, I wish the CPSU Presidium and Comrade Gorbachev personally, the best of success in their new policy." With that interview, Dubček broke a silence that had lasted almost 20 years, and the event did not pass unnoticed. His words were translated and published in major international newspapers, including the British *Guardian* and the West German *Die Zeit*.

Gustav Husák, now Czechoslovakia's president as well as party leader, also saw the similarities between perestroika and Prague Spring. But he was far less enthusiastic. For two decades, Husák had staked his claim to power in Czechoslovakia by maintaining that Alexander Dubček's reforms were a perversion of socialism. With reforms similar to Dubček's now emanating from the Kremlin, the citadel of orthodox communism, Husák's position was tenuous at best.

While remaining president, Husák stepped down as party leader. Milos Jakes, a conservative hard-liner who had been instrumental in dismantling the Prague Spring reforms, took over in December 1987. But little really changed: Freedom of expression was still limited, and dissidents who demonstrated for the government to uphold its own laws by respecting human rights were still arrested and imprisoned. Playwright Václav Havel, for example, who had emerged as the unofficial leader of the dissident movement, had spent four years in and out of prison.

State police in Prague form a blockade against demonstrators in 1989. With reform rapidly taking place in the Soviet Union under Gorbachev's direction, the spirit of Prague Spring rose again in Czechoslovakia that year. This time, the Czechoslovak people would not be denied.

On August 20, 1988, the 20th anniversary of the Soviet invasion of Czechoslovakia was marked by a demonstration of about 10,000 people in Prague. They were unhindered for about 30 minutes, but thereafter police arrested several demonstrators.

Though Dubček did not take part in this or any other demonstration, he cautiously began giving interviews once more. He even traveled to the University of Bologna, Italy, for a speaking engagement in November 1988. It was the first time he had left Czechoslovakia since 1970, and although cautious in what he said — he did not want the authorities in Prague to have any excuse to keep him from reentering the country — he nevertheless vigorously defended the reforms of Prague Spring. He reportedly told the Italian university officials, "I want to be rehabilitated, in all its effects — politically and . . . morally. . . . I don't want to be cited in scholastic textbooks and in encyclopedias as an ill-omened traitor who brought his country to ruin."

A protester is arrested by four riot policemen in Prague in October 1989. The man was one of some 10,000 antigovernment demonstrators to gather in Wenceslas Square and shout protests on the 71st anniversary of Czechoslovak independence.

Dubček was to get his wish the following year. Throughout 1989, there were signs that a major reassessment of Brezhnev's policies was under way in the Soviet Union. Articles appeared there that cast Dubček in a positive light. If the Soviets were rehabilitating Dubček, the suggestion was that Czechoslovakia's leaders should do the same.

But they did not, and soon it was too late. In mid-November 1989, the Prague police brutally assaulted some 25,000 student demonstrators on Milos Jakes's orders. Throughout the year, Communists had been pushed from power in Hungary, Poland, Bulgaria, and East Germany. Now the student demonstration precipitated a similar crisis in Czechoslovakia. For days after the event, hundreds of thousands of people poured into Prague's streets demanding an end to Communist rule. Soon the entire Czechoslovak Presidium, including Jakes, was forced to resign. At that point, Dubček appeared in public before the Czechoslovak people for the first time in 20 years. A new opposition movement, Civic Forum, headed by veteran dissidents, quickly formed. Václav Havel was its leader.

In November 1989, more than 100,000 people rallied for the Czechoslovak opposition movement and its principal organizational body, the Civic Forum. The group's leader, Václav Havel, and Alexander Dubček addressed the masses, calling for free speech and other democratic reforms.

Václav Havel, in and out of prison for 20 years while his plays were banned in his native country, became interim president of Czechoslovakia in December 1989. Dubček, the man who led his country part of the way down the road to democracy in the 1960s, became chairman of the Federal Assembly, and a new day dawned for Czechoslovakia.

Throughout December 1989, Civic Forum engaged in tough negotiations with the Communists, demanding that they give up not only their monopoly on power but also their "leading role." Paralyzed and isolated, Czechoslovakia's leadership had no other choice but to give in. For the first time since

1948, non-Communists were admitted into government, and Gustav Husák was forced to swear in to official positions many people whom he had previously imprisoned. Husák resigned from the presidency on December 10, but not before the government was forced to admit that the 1968 invasion of Czechoslovakia had been a mistake.

A plan was worked out for free elections to be held within a year. Havel agreed to serve as interim president, and Dubček agreed to act as chairman of the Federal Assembly. On Thursday, December 28, 1989, Dubček was unanimously elected by the Assembly's 303 voters to the chairmanship, the same job he had held during those few months before leaving public life in 1969.

The world that Stalin created in the wake of World War II, when he forcibly imposed his version of communism on the people of Eastern Europe, lasted for almost 45 years. In that time, Communist control had been absolute. But the people of Eastern Europe never accepted the repressive system that crushed them. When Mikhail Gorbachev began to dismantle Stalin's legacy, it did not take long for the discredited regimes to fall. In 1989, the Communist monopoly on power in Eastern Europe was wrested away in Poland, Hungary, East Germany, Bulgaria, Czechoslovakia, and Romania. Communist dictators either voluntarily resigned or were ousted, arrested, or — as in the case of Romania's unrepentant Nicolae Ceaușescu, who had ordered his private security police to massacre thousands of civilians — killed. People had had enough of the Communist version of tyranny.

One Communist, Alexander Dubček, still had the loyalty of the Czechoslovak people. In 40 years he had been the only Czechoslovak Communist leader to place the needs and aspirations of his people above personal power and party dogma. As numerous Communist officials, many of them his former colleagues, were banished from power in 1989, Dubček reemerged from the shadows to unify and lead. The socialist with a human face was for his people a symbol of a brief but bright moment in a nation's long, dark past. Now he belonged to the future.

> *I do not think we can win over the younger generation by reproaching it or by telling it that everything it enjoys had to be won by hard effort. The enthusiasm of our youth cannot be restricted to praising our own achievements. Our young people want to have achievements of their own.*
> —ALEXANDER DUBČEK

Further Reading

Chapman, Colin. *August 21st: The Rape of Czechoslovakia.* Philadelphia: Lippincott, 1968.

Heller, Mikhail, and Aleksandr Nekrich. *Utopia in Power: The History of the Soviet Union from 1917 to the Present.* New York: Simon & Schuster, 1986.

Lewis, Gavin. *Tomáš Masaryk.* New York: Chelsea House, 1990.

Mlynar, Zdenek. *Night Frost in Prague: The End of Humane Socialism.* London: C. Hurst & Company, 1980.

Navazelskis, Ina. *Leonid Brezhnev.* New York: Chelsea House, 1988.

Saxon-Ford, Stephanie. *The Czech Americans.* New York: Chelsea House, 1989.

Shawcross, William. *Dubček.* New York: Simon & Schuster, 1970.

Skilling, H. Gordon. *Czechoslovakia's Interrupted Revolution.* Princeton, NJ: Princeton University Press, 1976.

Stolarik, M. Mark. *The Slovak Americans.* New York: Chelsea House, 1988.

Szulc, Tad. *Czechoslovakia Since World War II.* New York: Viking, 1971.

Chronology

Nov. 27, 1921	Born Alexander Dubček in Uhrovec, Slovakia
1938–39	Munich agreement; Germany occupies Czechoslovakia and invades Poland, beginning World War II; Dubček joins Communist party
1944–48	Allies liberate Czechoslovakia; World War II ends; Dubček marries Anna Ondrisova; takes job in Trenčín yeast factory; organizes Communist party activities; Communists gain control of Czechoslovakia
1949–59	Dubček named district party secretary in Trenčín; appointed regional party secretary for Banská Bystrica; attends Higher Party School in Moscow; graduates with a doctorate in political science; returns to Czechoslovakia; named first secretary of the Slovak Communist party in Bratislava
1960–67	Climbs party ranks and forms power base
1968	Replaces Antonín Novotný as first secretary of the Czechoslovak Communist party; institutes democratic reforms; Prague Spring; 200,000 Warsaw Pact troops invade Czechoslovakia; Dubček and other top aides arrested
1969	Gustav Husák replaces Dubček as first secretary; Dubček becomes chairman of the Federal Assembly; Prague demonstrations marking first anniversary of Soviet invasion result in violence; Dubček enacts Emergency Laws, suspending civil liberties
1970–81	Expelled from Communist party; becomes mechanic for the Forestry Department in Bratislava; retires
1985	Mikhail Gorbachev becomes first secretary of the Communist party of the Soviet Union; introduces perestroika and glasnost
Dec. 1987	Milos Jakes succeeds Husák
Aug. 1988	10,000 people demonstrate in Prague to mark the 20th anniversary of the Soviet invasion
Nov. 1988	Dubček lectures in Italy
1989	Soviet Union begins reassessment of 1968 invasion of Czechoslovakia; Communist governments forced to share power in Poland, Hungary, East Germany, Romania, and Bulgaria
Nov. 1989	25,000 demonstrators in Prague are brutally beaten; numerous other demonstrations ensue; Czechoslovak government is forced to resign; Dubček appears in public in Czechoslovakia for the first time in 20 years; Civic Forum and its leader, Václav Havel, emerge as opposition gains momentum
Dec. 1989	Civic Forum negotiates power away from the Communists; Havel elected interim president; Dubček elected chairman of Federal Assembly; free elections planned within one year

Index

Kundera, Milan, 64, 77
Lenin, Vladimir Ilyich Ulyanov, 22, 55, 97
Liberman, Evsei, 63
Literary Listy, 77
Literary Noviny, 77
L' Unita, 102
Margolius, Heda, 49–50
Margolius, Rudolf, 49
Marx, Karl, 17–18, 55
May Day, 83
Masaryk, Jan, 41, 49
Masaryk, Tomáš, 19, 25, 48, 78
Mauthausen, 31, 32
Mlynar, Zdenek, 72
Mnacko, Ladislav, 64
Moscow, 55–57
Munich agreement, 28
Nagy, Imre, 57, 81
National Front, 38, 59
National Socialist party, 26
New York Times, 69
North Atlantic Treaty Organization
    (NATO), 37
Novotný, Antonín, 53, 58–59, 60, 63–66,
    67, 70, 71, 72, 74, 80
Palach, Jan, 96
Perestroika, 101, 102
Piller, Jan, 80
Pishpek, 20–22
Prace, 77
Prague Spring, 14, 76–81, 95, 99, 103, 104
Pravda, 95
Purges, 45–51, 65
Roosevelt, Franklin, 35

Rude Pravo, 49
Sik, Ota, 63–64, 72
Siroky, Viliam, 31, 53
Slánský, Rudolf, 48, 51, 53, 78
Slovak Communist party, 29–30, 43, 47
Slovak National Council, 60
Smidke, Karol, 51
Smrkovsky, Josef, 72, 90
Soviet Union, 14, 15, 19–21, 22–23, 27, 28,
    32, 35–39, 43, 45, 51, 55, 56–57, 63,
    64, 65, 72, 86, 89, 90, 93, 95, 101
Spacek, Josef, 72
Stalin, Joseph, 23, 28, 31, 35–37, 38, 43,
    45–51, 83, 102
Svoboda, Ludvík, 72, 92
Szulc, Tad, 69
Tito, Josip Broz, 47, 83
Transcarpathia, 38
2,000 Words, The (Vaculik), 87–88
Uhrovec, 15
Ulbricht, Walter, 72
Union of Czech Writers, 77
United States, 17, 35
Vaculik, Ludvík, 64, 86–87
Warsaw Letter, 88
Warsaw Treaty Organization (Warsaw Pact),
    37, 57, 81, 87, 89, 91
Wilson, Woodrow, 15
World War I, 15, 16, 19, 25, 26
World War II, 28, 31, 32–33, 72, 81
Yalta Conference, 35–36
Yugloslavia, 47
Zápotocký, Antonín, 53
Zhivkov, Todor, 73

Ina L. Navazelskis is the author of numerous books and articles on Eastern European affairs, including *Leonid Brezhnev* in the Chelsea House series WORLD LEADERS — PAST & PRESENT. A graduate of the London School of Economics and the Columbia University School of Journalism, she has traveled extensively in Eastern Europe and has been active internationally in the cause of human rights.

Arthur M. Schlesinger, jr., taught history at Harvard for many years and is currently Albert Schweitzer Professor of the Humanities at City University of New York. He is the author of numerous highly praised works in American history and has twice been awarded the Pulitzer Prize. He served in the White House as special assistant to Presidents Kennedy and Johnson.

PICTURE CREDITS

Anonymous: pp. 23, 39, 52; AP/Wide World Photos: pp. 30, 40, 42, 47, 48, 61, 62, 82, 89, 91, 94, 102, 104, 105; The Bettmann Archive: pp. 16, 18, 27, 41; Goess/SIPA-PRESS: pp. 2, 74–75, 88, 98–99; Keystone: pp. 84–85; Library of Congress: p. 36 (neg. # USZ62-7449); Institute for Democracy in Eastern Europe: p. 103; Langevin/SYGMA: p. 100; Kraysztof Miller: p. 106; Reuter/Bettmann Archive: pp. 12, 14; Sipahioglu/SIPA-PRESS: p. 93; SIPA-PRESS: p. 71; UPI/Bettmann Archive: pp. 15, 21, 22, 24, 28, 29, 33, 34, 44, 46, 49, 50, 54–55, 56, 58, 66, 68, 73, 76, 79, 90, 92, 96; WWII Pictorial Collection, Hoover Institution Archives, Stanford University: p. 31

Every effort has been made to contact the copyright owners of photos and illustrations in this book. If the holder of the copyright of a photograph in this book has not heard from us, he or she should contact Chelsea House.

3 9507 0000 4451 0

WITHDRAWN

YA
B—DUBCEK
Navazelskis, In
Alexander Dubc

YA
B—DUBCEK
Navazelskis, Ina L.
Alexander Dubcek.

17.95

MAR 22

12-143